Adventist Online Education:
Realizing the Potential

Adventist Online Education: Realizing the Potential

Edited by
Janine M. Lim and Anthony Williams

Avondale
ACADEMIC PRESS

Avondale Academic Press
PO Box 19
Cooranbong NSW 2265
Australia
www.avondale.edu.au/research/avondale-academic-press

Layout: Miriam Kingston

Cataloguing in publication data may be found at:
http://catalogue.nla.gov.au/

ISBN:
Paperback 978-0-9876392-2-6
Kindle eBook 978-0-9876392-3-3

Contents

Effectiveness

List of Figures

List of Tables

Introduction

Janine Lim. Associate Dean, Online Higher Education; Professor,
Educational Technology, Andrews University, Berrien Springs,
United States

Anthony Williams. Director of Academic Governance and Performance,
The University of Wollongong Global Enterprises, Wollongong, Australia.
Adjunct Professor, Avondale College of Higher Education, Cooranbong,
Australia.

Adventist online education has been growing since the 1990s. This collection of research is a step forward, the first time Adventist research in the strategies, methods, techniques, and tools of online learning have been shared in this method. We celebrate the achievements of our institutions in continuous learning and improvement in the delivery of Adventist education online, while looking forward to realizing the full potential of online education to reach more students with the unique experiences and benefits of Adventist education.

From the early 1900s, educators were working to ensure all students had access to Adventist education. In 1909, Frederick Griggs established The Fireside Correspondence School to provide the benefits of an Adventist education to those unable to attend traditional schools. Those early days of distance education via the correspondence method grew by leaps and bounds in the first decade of the Internet, with Andrews University, Adventist International Institute of Advanced Studies, Loma Linda University, Southern Adventist University, and University of Montemorelos beginning online and distributed education degrees. The need for collaboration and networking to enhance the quality and depth of distance education began with a partnership in 1969 between Home Study Institute and Columbia Union College for the first distance education consortium in the Adventist system. Then in 1999, a group of mainly faculty met in Florida to discuss the "burning platform" and necessity of collaboration and change, starting what became the Adventist Virtual Learning Network. As Adventist online education continues to grow, the possibilities of technology to provide additional opportunities for sharing and collaboration have captured the interest of Adventist educators. In

October 2017, the research papers in this collection, as well as many practical sessions, were shared at the Adventist Online Learning Conference in Berrien Springs, Michigan. Networking and learning from each other continue to be essential for our collective success.

The 2017 Adventist Online Learning Conference was designed and planned in the spirit of the Adventist Virtual Learning Network conferences, which were coordinated and hosted throughout the North American Division from 1999 through 2006. In 2005, AVLN coordinated the first Adventist conference on distance education totally online; and in 2006, AVLN coordinated the first bilingual Adventist conference on distance education, totally online, in partnership with the University of Montemorelos. The Adventist Online Learning Conference was co-hosted by Andrews University, Griggs International Academy, and the University of Montemorelos. Griggs International Academy coordinated and hosted live Facebook streaming as well as onsite sessions supporting K-12 online education. And on the higher education side, a rich collection of sessions and research papers were shared from a variety of institutions. Participants, both onsite and virtual, came from Australia, Austria, Brazil, Canada, Columbia, Jamaica, Mexico, New Zealand, Philippines, United Kingdom, and the United States. Participation was strong, with 79 presenters, 124 attendees in Michigan, and 73 virtual attendees. Partnerships included sponsorship by the Adventist Learning Community, the Inter-American Division of Seventh-day Adventists, and the North American Division of Seventh-day Adventists. In addition, partnership with Avondale College of Higher Education resulted in research papers presented at the conference, culminating in this publication.

This research spans four major areas of online delivery in Adventist education: (1) most importantly, the pursuit of Adventist distinctiveness and the Adventist experience within online delivery; (2) the empowering and enabling of students, staff, and faculty for advising, monitoring, and resourcing quality online experiences; (3) the power of technology to support collaboration among our institutions, our faculty, our teams; and (4) the supports, training, and methods needed for the effectiveness of online delivery. With this research comes an invitation to join the conversation, improving and growing the quality of Adventist online delivery. We invite you to participate in the monthly meetings of the Adventist Distance Education Professionals. See https://www.andrews.edu/distance/partnerships/adep/ for details.

Janine Lim

Janine Lim currently serves as associate dean for online higher education and professor of educational technology in the School of Distance Education and International Partnerships at Andrews University, in Berrien Springs, Michigan. She and her team support over 300 online courses, provide training for faculty teaching online, and work with the campus infrastructure support of online learning. Her department also provides educational technology and Moodle support for faculty and students. In addition, Janine is responsible for the faculty and courses of the Consortium of Adventist Colleges and Universities. Janine has taught over 15 unique graduate educational technology classes online numerous times over the past two decades, with some classes attracting participants from all over the world. Her undergraduate teaching includes social media courses for communication and digital media majors. Janine has served on the board of the United States Distance Learning Association since April 2015. Prior to her work at Andrews University, Janine coordinated distance education for 22 K-12 school districts in southwest Michigan for 14 years. In that position, she won several awards for educational technology and distance education, and co-founded TWICE (Two-Way Interactive Connections in Education), Michigan's K-12 Videoconferencing Organization. Her research interests include successful online teacher behaviors, quality online discussions, and student activity patterns in self-paced courses.

Anthony Williams

Anthony Williams recently joined the University of Wollongong Global Enterprises Unit. The unit manages universities and colleges in four locations in Wollongong, Dubai, Hong Kong and Malaysia. Anthony manages the Academic Governance and Performance Portfolio across the institutions. Before taking up the Wollongong assignment, he was at Avondale where he was Vice President (Academic and Research) of Avondale College of Higher Education. He provided leadership in research and scholarship. Prior to that role, he held the position of the Head of School of Architecture and Built Environment at the University of Newcastle NSW. He has extensive experience in project management in the domain of professional education. He is a winner of multiple University Teaching Awards as well as a National Award for Teaching Excellence. He is highly regarded in this area having worked as a curriculum consultant nationally and internationally.

List of Contributors

Janine Lim. Associate Dean, Online Higher Education; Professor, Educational Technology, Andrews University, Berrien Springs, United States. Corresponding Author: janine@andrews.edu.

Anthony Williams. Director of Academic Governance and Performance, The University of Wollongong Global Enterprises, Wollongong, Australia. Adjunct Professor, Avondale College of Higher Education, Cooranbong, Australia.

Leni Casimiro. Director of AIIAS Online. Adventist International Institute of Advanced Studies, Silang, Cavite, Philippines. Corresponding Author: leni@aiias.edu.

Safary Wa-Mbaleka. Associate Professor, Education Department. Adventist International Institute of Advanced Studies, Silang, Philippines. Corresponding Author: wa-mbalekas@aiias.edu.

Glynis Bradfield. Director of Undergraduate Distance Student Services. Andrews University, Berrien Springs, United States. Corresponding Author: glynisb@andrews.edu.

Maria Northcote. Director of the Centre for Advancement of the Scholarship of Teaching and Learning. Avondale College of Higher Education, Cooranbong, Australia. Corresponding Author: maria.northcote@avondale.edu.au.

Kevin Petrie. Dean of the Faculty of Education, Business and Science. Avondale College of Higher Education, Cooranbong, Australia.

John Seddon. Research Project Manager. Avondale College of Higher Education, Cooranbong, Australia.

Sherene Hattingh. Primary Education Course Convenor, Faculty of Education, Business and Science. Avondale College of Higher Education, Cooranbong, Australia.

John Reddin. Director of Operations mobileLearning.io, North Ryde, Australia.

Carolina Costa Cavalcanti. Professor. Adventist University of São Paulo (UNASP). Corresponding Author: carolina.cavalcanti@ucb.org.br.

Everson Muckenberger. Academic Manager. Adventist University of São Paulo (UNASP).

Andrea Filatro. Speaker, author and researcher in Instructional Design. Adventist University of São Paulo (UNASP).

Robert A. Paulson. Professor of Exercise Science. Pacific Union College, Angwin, United States. Corresponding Author: bpaulson@puc.edu.

Shirley Freed. Chair, School of Education. Burman University, Lacombe, Canada.

David A. Jeffrey. Assistant Professor, Business. Burman University, Lacombe, Canada. Corresponding Author: david.jeffrey@gmail.com.

Randy J. Siebold. Associate Professor, Leadership. Andrews University, Berrien Springs, United States.

Nancy Liliana Herrera Villamizar. Coordinator of Planning and Academic Management. University of Montemorelos, Montemorelos, Mexico. Corresponding Author: lherreradec@um.edu.mx.

Dora Patricia Martínez Cebreros. Coordinator of Student and Faculty Services. University of Montemorelos, Montemorelos, Mexico.

Caterina Evelin Pavoni. Online Quality Assurance. University of Montemorelos, Montemorelos, Mexico.

Prema Gaikwad. Professor, Education Department. Adventist International Institute of Advance Studies, Silang, Philippines. Corresponding Author: pgaikwad@aiias.edu.

Mak Chung Yin. Senior Doctoral Student, Education Department. Adventist International Institute of Advance Studies, Silang, Philippines

Adventist Distinctiveness

Since the first meeting of the Adventist Virtual Learning Lab in the North American Division in 1999, keeping Adventist online education uniquely Adventist has been a key concern of Adventist educators at all levels. In this section, educators from the Adventist International Institute of Advanced Studies, in Silang, Philippines share their research in how our faith and mission informs our online practice. Leni Casimiro explores how a mission focus can be evident throughout a variety of disciplines taught online. Safary Wa-Mbaleka explores the student perspectives of a great Christian facilitator of online courses.

1. Is Mission Possible Online? Exploring Mission-Oriented Online Course Designs

Leni Casimiro. Director of AIIAS Online. Adventist International Institute of Advanced Studies, Silang, Cavite, Philippines. Corresponding Author: leni@aiias.edu

Abstract

Adventist schools have a mission to fulfil in response to Christ's commission. In reality, however, integrating mission activities in online classes remains a challenge. A review of 10 online courses showed that there are four approaches to mission-oriented course designs that can be employed in online education. The resulting Mission Integration Model provided the components of a mission-oriented online course, consisting of the course design approaches and related outcomes.

The Challenge of Adventist Online Education

Adventism's reason for existence is mission, and mission is the reason for Adventist online education. If online learning cannot accomplish the church's mission, there is no reason for it to exist in its schools. George Knight, foremost church historian and philosopher, puts it strongly by calling this mission-to-the-world orientation the "Adventist educational imperative" (Knight, 2017, p. 4). It is only by responding to God's Great Commission that Adventist education, whether on-site or online, can achieve its purpose.

With the exponential growth of knowledge in this information age, it is easy for a teacher, particularly in higher education, to get entangled with the enormity and complexity of information that needs to be acquired. Without conscious attention, focusing on too many details can distract one from the big picture, the biblical worldview, in class lessons. Without intentionality, the goal to master higher order academic skills can set aside the real purpose of Adventist education—the preparation for engagement in God's Great Commission. Adventist schools are therefore given the mandate to consciously and intentionally become mission-oriented.

Adventist schools are gifted with a rich literature on integration of faith and learning (IFL) in the writings of Ellen White. Emphasis on the development of a biblical worldview and Christian values in students has been given. The significant role of a Christian teacher in the character formation of students has always been underscored. School campuses are expected to prepare spiritual master plans that involve students in mission-related activities. One can only expect the best if such injunctions are fully implemented in every school.

The entry of online learning into the educational system, however, has created a stir among Adventist education circles. How can IFL be done effectively if the school has no control of the student's context? How can teachers function as role models if they are geographically distant from students? How can online students engage in the school's mission activities if they are not on campus? Can the development of Christian worldview, character, and values be mediated by technology?

Compounding the IFL challenge are the commonly held practices among online education circles. Because of the distance between teachers and online students, course content and learning activities are delivered mainly through text or videos, deficient of personal touch. Learning becomes self-directed and almost always independent while the teacher role is conceived in instructional terms such as design, facilitation, and direct instruction such that the teacher's personal influence is greatly diminished (Garrison & Anderson, 2003; Preisman, 2014; Sheridan & Kelly, 2010). It is common to see online courses that merely address the cognitive aspect, making them more appealing to intellectual development than character formation (Jung, 2015). It is much easier, for example, to talk about possible mission outreach activities than to be involved in them in an online class.

Considering the challenges faced by online education, there is therefore a great need to identify ways that will transform a regular online classroom into one that is truly Adventist. This study is an attempt to discover effective approaches in creating mission-oriented online courses, particularly in higher education. Specifically, it focused on answering the question: How should online courses be designed to engage students in missions? This study aimed to contribute to the scanty researched-based literature on mission-oriented online course designs.

Literature Review

The Great Commission and Adventist Education

A review of the history of Adventist education reveals its close affinity with the church's work on mission. According to Knight (2017), "the foremost purpose of the denomination's early educational enterprise was to train men and women to spread the three angels' messages" (p. 5). Because of this, Knight observes, "modern Adventism views (or should view) its massive educational system as a major arm of its missiological endeavor" (p. 5).

For Adventists, the aim of true education goes beyond mere academic preparation. It is the "harmonious development of the physical, the mental, and the spiritual powers" of the students as it prepares them "for the joy of service in this world and for the higher joy of wider service in the world to come" (White, 2002, p. 13). In line with this, the General Conference Education Department's (2003) statement on the aim and mission of Adventist education says,

> Adventist education prepares students for a useful and joy-filled life, fostering friendship with God, whole-person development, Bible-based values, and *selfless service in accordance with the Seventh-day Adventist mission to the world.* (p. 221)

There is no question that Adventist education works hand in hand with the church's mission. It originated in response to mission and continues to exist to fulfil God's Great Commission. As a training ground for mission involvement, Adventist schools do not just remain in the awareness level of the church's mission activities but provide students with actual experiences until they develop the commitment to engage in them. In *Counsels to Parents, Teachers, and Students*, White (2011) said, "They [students] are not to look forward to a time, after the school term closes, when they will do some large work for God, but should study how, during their student life, to yoke up with Christ in unselfish service for others." This involvement, White adds, can help the students "take a broad view of their present obligations to God" (p. 547).

Mission in the Integration of Faith and Learning

Mission-related activities in schools are usually considered part of IFL. Research on IFL practices in higher education, however, appears to give emphasis on gaining Christian perspective, developing Christian values, teacher-student relations, and school atmosphere (Ponyatovska, 2015; Trye, 2017). Applied IFL strategies lean heavily toward content and school context while mission to the world is left out. This is not to say that schools of higher learning are not doing mission activities. The surveyed teachers did not cite them probably because such activities are part of the co-curricular activities, which are usually apart from academic departments, conducted school-wide, and participated in on a voluntary basis.

Part of the outcomes of Adventist tertiary education, according to the General Conference, is for its students to "answer God's call in the selection and pursuit of their chosen careers, *in selfless service to the mission of the Church,* and in building a free, just, and productive society and world community" (GC Policy Manual, 2003, para 26). This calls schools to be more intentional in integrating mission in their IFL strategies. As an enabling agency for the Great Commission, every student must be seen as a potential disciple of Jesus and thus must be given all the necessary training.

In an attempt to give a solution to the looming crisis that is being experienced by Adventist schools, Anderson (2009) underscored the importance of "instilling passion for the unique mission of the Adventist Church" (p. 112). How is this done? Anderson suggested, among options, that "whenever possible, have students bring the unique Adventist message and mission into contact with real life . . . . *But you've got to make it real, hands-on,* not just theory taught in the classroom" (p. 113). This means providing students opportunities to engage in actual mission activities.

Faith and Learning Integration in Online Education

Faith integration strategies in online classrooms are not completely different from those in traditional campuses. A survey of IFL strategies used in an online environment revealed three categories, namely, instructional, relational, and environmental strategies (Casimiro, 2013). Just as in face-to-face settings, enriching content with biblical principles, maintaining healthy web-based relationships through learning communities, and providing a strong spiritual component in course designs were considered important. Because of the distance factor, however, teacher presence (particularly through forum facilitation), contextualization of learning experiences, and the importance of strong student support were emphasized in the online environment.

Again, just as in face-to-face settings, mission was not cited among the IFL strategies in the online environment, although it could have been present in some courses.

Designing Instruction for Mission

If involvement in mission is the goal of the school, it should be seen in every school activity. After all, both the work of redemption and restoration of God's lost image in man, which are repeatedly emphasized by Ellen White as the object of education (White, 2002), are essentially the focus of mission work. This means mission-oriented projects will not be just one of the options among co-curricular activities of the school. Rather, every school activity, curricular or co-curricular, becomes mission-oriented (du Preez, 2001). Mission becomes an essential part of learning in whichever delivery format—face-to-face, online, or blended—is used in class.

In order to create a desire among students to get involved in missions, it is important that learning goes beyond head knowledge. According to Jung (2015), "the ability to form students' character depends on whether thoughts reach the level of emotion in the heart. *Formational learning* requires emotions to be involved, bringing greater value to what we understand, which prompts change . . . . How we feel about what we think has great potential for what we do" (p. 54).

Having a desire to do something, however, does not automatically lead to doing it well. Particularly when skills are called for, students need to be given opportunities to exercise them so they can be prepared to face the real world (Fry, Ketteridge, & Marshall, 2009). This underscores the importance of active engagement in learning, which is foundational to many theories of learning such as *learning-by-doing* (Reese, 2011*)*, *experiential learning* (Kolb, 1984), and *active learning* (Eison, 2010). Service learning is another strategy that can be applied to mission engagement because of its inherent assumption that involvement in community service enriches what is learned in the classroom (Hebert & Hauf, 2015).

Finally, the challenges posed by distance and technology-mediated learning in online education highlight the value of intentional learning in mission integration. According to Blumschein (2012), "in contrast to latent or incidental learning, intentional learning is generally defined as learning that is motivated by intentions and is goal directed" (p. 1600). If the goals of Adventist education are to be achieved, teachers have to be intentional in integrating mission and this has to be made part of the student's cognitive orientation (Bereiter & Scardamalia, as cited in Blumschein, 2012).

The lack of literature that deals specifically with mission-oriented online course designs underscores the need for this study. Nevertheless, as mission is much a part of IFL, faith integration principles can serve as the analytical tool in evaluating mission integration practices in actual online classrooms.

Methodology

To find out how mission is effectively integrated into online course design necessitated the use of documentary analysis (Bowen, 2009; Payne & Payne, 2004; Scott, 1990) of all teacher and student-generated materials in each of the selected online classes. Documents examined included the syllabus, the content, learning activities (projects, assignments, etc.), the discussion forums, and the devotional sections of each course. Since the courses were delivered fully online and were kept intact in the learning management system, all course materials, including class interactions, were available for analysis.

The use of actual course materials fulfils Scott's (1990) quality control criteria such as authenticity, credibility, representativeness, and meaning for handling documentary sources. The course materials were authentic because they were all primary documents, accessed through the archived actual course webpages in the school's learning management system. The courses were credible because they were developed, offered, and completed prior to, independently, and not for the benefit of this research. In addition, looking into both teacher and student-generated course materials for the purpose of data triangulation contributed to the credibility of the analysis.

Representativeness and meaning were established by selecting courses that were supportive of mission in the IFL literature and the Adventist philosophy of education. Since the study attempted to discover mission-oriented course designs, it was deemed necessary that only courses that showed mission orientation be included. To achieve this, all the 36 fully online courses that were offered from school years 2014-2015 to 2016-2017 in the graduate school of one higher education institution were subjected to a preliminary screening process.

Screening for inclusion in the study was carried out by looking for mission-related content and learning activities in the course materials.

The courses were rated on a scale of 0 to 5 on the extent of inclusion of mission, with 0 having none and 5 having the most number of mission oriented content and activities. All courses that received the highest rate were selected, resulting in a total of ten courses that were subjected to a more detailed documentary analysis. Of this ten, four came from the field of education, four from public health, and two from business.

In the coding process during documentary analysis, interpretation of data was based on IFL principles and the Adventist philosophy of education, particularly its emphasis on Adventism's role in spreading the gospel to all the world. As this is a qualitative research study, the primary tool for data analysis was the researcher. Being a born Adventist and an experienced educator in Adventist schools, both online and onsite, the researcher interpreted the data through the lens of an Adventist perspective. Triangulation of findings rested on the multiplicity of data sources, the inclusion of three different programs of study, and the use of both teacher- and student-generated documents.

Presentation and Discussion of Findings

Initial coding of mission-related content and activities in the ten online courses that were selected for the study revealed six integration strategies, namely, *worship, Christian perspective, information, awareness, response,* and *engagement.* Coding was based on the focus and description of each of the strategies as shown in Table 1.1.

Table 1.1 Initial Categories of Mission Integration

Mission Integration Strategies	Document Source	Focus	Description
Worship	• Devotional Message & Forum	God	• Jesus Christ is acknowledged as the model for acts of service, the true missionary
Christian Perspective	• Course Content • Discussion Forums • Course Syllabus	Worldview	• Topics in class are seen from the point of view of their role in accomplishing the church's mission
Information	• Course Content • Discussion Forums • Course Syllabus	Knowledge	• Mission is integrated as topics in the content but no response required of the student. • Information about church mission is shared in class.

Mission Integration Strategies	Document Source	Focus	Description
Awareness	• Course Content • Discussion Forums • Assignment	Mission opportunities	• Teacher raises awareness of students on the many opportunities to engage in missions. • Students express the importance or value of participation in mission. • Teacher or students share mission stories.
Response	• Discussion Forums • Assignment	Personal response	• Teacher calls for participation in mission but no actual engagement is required. • Students express willingness to participate in mission.
Engagement	• Discussion Forums • Assignment • Course Syllabus	Action	• Students are asked to act on a mission.

As can be seen in the summary of the initial coding process in Table 1.2, some strategies appeared closely related both in occurrence and focus, hence the need to combine them.

Table 1.2 Mission Integration Strategies by Course and Program

Strategies	Education				Public Health				Business	
	Course 1	Course 2	Course 3	Course 4	Course 5	Course 6	Course 7	Course 8	Course 9	Course 10
Worship	✓	✓	✓	✓	✓	✓	✓	✓	✓	✓
Christian Perspective	✓	✓	-	✓	✓	-	-	✓	-	-
Information	✓	✓	-	-	✓	-	-	✓	-	-
Awareness	✓	✓	✓	✓	✓	✓	✓	-	-	-
Response	✓	✓	✓	✓	✓	-	-	-	✓	✓
Engagement	✓	✓	-	-	✓	✓	✓	✓	-	-

Using further recursive abstraction, the data were reduced to four categories. Inclusion of mission topics (coded 'information') in the content is also done when approaching content with 'Christian perspective,' hence the two were combined under a 'worldview' category. Also combined under a new category, 'character formation,' were 'awareness' and 'response' as they both focused on developing love for mission in students. Worship was retained while 'engagement' was renamed to 'service' to clarify the kind of tasks expected of the students when engaged in mission. Table 1.3 presents the final four categories, now called approaches to mission integration, and their goals as used in the coding process.

Table 1.3 Approaches to Mission Integration

Final Categories	Initial Categories	Goal
Worship	• Worship	To provide the context for spiritual maturity to take place so students can commit to participate in His mission.
Cognitive/ Worldview	• Christian Perspective • Information	To set the course within the context of the church's mission and let the students see how a specific course topic can contribute to the fulfil-ment of this mission.
Character For-mation	• Awareness • Response	To inculcate love for people and missions through activities that allow them to make decisions on what to do and reflect on their choices.
Service	• Engagement	To give students opportunities to engage in actual missions.

Based on the summary of the final coding process (see Table 1.4) conducted on the courses, it was evident that Worship, followed by Character Formation, were the most popular strategies to integrate mission in the classes. About half of the courses utilized Service and Worldview approaches in their designs. How the courses utilized these approaches is the focus of the next section.

Table 1.4 Mission Integration Approaches by Course and Program

Approaches	Education				Public Health				Business	
	Course 1	Course 2	Course 3	Course 4	Course 5	Course 6	Course 7	Course 8	Course 9	Course 10
Worship	✓	✓	✓	✓	✓	✓	✓	✓	✓	✓
Cognitive/ Worldview	✓	✓	-	✓	✓	-	-	✓	-	-
Character Formation	✓	✓	✓	✓	✓	✓	✓	-	✓	✓
Service	✓	✓	-	-	✓	✓	✓	✓	-	-

The Four Mission-Oriented Course Designs

The resulting mission-oriented course designs were utilized in the online courses in varying degrees and combinations. As evidences of usage ranged from simple citations in the course syllabus to lengthy lecture pages, only a sampling of each approach is shown in this section.

Worship. Worship appeared to be the easiest approach to use as it only involved the preparation of a devotional message, accompanied by a discussion forum. It doesn't require major adjustments in the course requirements nor the course content. Since the respondent institution requires inclusion of devotional activities in all its online courses, all the courses examined showed at least one mission-related devotional and thus were positive in the worship approach. This approach seem compatible with courses that are heavy in technical content or that rely on huge amounts of content that is written by secular authors—a common occurrence in graduate education, especially in the fields of business, science, and health. An example of this approach can be seen in an excerpt of the Meditation Forum of one business class (Course 10):

> **Week 1: Jesus as Marketer**
>
> Have you thought of "marketing in a Biblical way"? To be more specific, do you think Jesus was a marketer? If He was, what was He marketing? What about His ethical practices in Marketing? What was the content of His marketing? Can He be considered an ethical marketer? As we begin this new learning journey, I would like us to root our learning upon the Bible, especially in Jesus' marketing methods. Jesus' marketing methods were very successful. Many people got to know Him and become [sic] His followers. In other words, or in a [sic] business terms, people bought the product of Jesus: the truth and the Gospel. All of us, who are reading this devotional thoughts [sic], are called to be partners with Jesus in His marketing – to identify people with unfulfilled needs and who desire the truth and the Gospel. Let us be an instrument of Jesus and be the salt and light of the world (Matthew 5:13-16).

Character Formation. Character formation was observed mostly in application types of class discussions, although it was sometimes seen in the content and assignment sections of the courses. In this approach, the teacher and/or students cite specific mission activities where class lessons may be applied, highlighted at times with stories of actual field experiences. The teacher may be intentional in encouraging students to participate in such mission activities. An indicator of its impact on students is seen most especially in their reflections either in the discussion area or in their journal. In some instances, the teacher uses case studies that lead to solutions that call for decisions that are mission-oriented. An example of a character formation approach can be seen in a forum discussion in course 5 when a student posted his planned ministry:

> For this I will do a house based Lifestyle session, they will come for a [sic] daily instruction to my house for one month, in that month, my family and I will provide fresh produce, groceries and all they need (on [sic] preparation for this my family and I decide to set 5% of our income aside every month for a "benevolence fund") so I can teach them how to implement the 8 laws of health in a very practical way.

and a classmate responded this way:

> … what a wonderful example of sacrifice to set aside a portion of your income in order to help others live more healthfully. Being in self-supporting work and living on a missionary income is already a sacrifice and you are going above and beyond that. Imagine if every church member were to follow your example. May God bless you and your family. Good program, too!

Cognitive or Worldview. Indicators of a worldview approach mostly involved relating class topics to church mission through a videotaped presentation of course content, a teacher-prepared supporting content page for a textbook-based course, or class discussion. Although worldview was an obvious approach to integrate mission, it was used only in 5 of the 10 courses observed for this study. It also appeared that the way the online classes integrated an Adventist perspective appeared mostly in the cognitive level, although worldview can go beyond mere cognitive orientation. The seeming difficulty of a worldview approach is probably due to the enormity of topics to be covered in class that necessitated the use of textbooks as well as the high level of technicality in class topics. An example of this approach was best utilized in Course 2, an education course, which was textbook-based but allotted the first unit to lay down the foundation of the course from an Adventist worldview. Figure 1.1 shows part of the first unit's front page, with its description.

Figure 1.1 Worldview example from Course 2

Unit 1

Introduction: Developing Teacher Expertise

July 11-15, 2016

The topic for this week lays down the foundation of the field of instructional supervision, its importance, and the purpose of its existence in schools, within the perspective of the Adventist philosophy of education. It identifies the conditions for the development of teacher expertise in order to enhance student achievement.

Service. Engaging the students in actual mission work as part of class activities was used in 6 of the 10 courses (see Table 1.4). This is the only approach that called for actual engagement in community outreach either through acts of service or evangelism. Service approach was observable in courses that (a) intentionally included mission-oriented outcomes in the course syllabus, (b) designed assignments that allowed students to engage in mission, and (c) provided for reflections on mission activities either in the written report on assignments, discussion area, or individual journals. An example of this approach is a course requirement in course 5 shown in Figure 1.2 that sends students to do service to their immediate community:

Figure 1.2 Service in the community from Course 5

APPLY (Day 5)

Health Ministry Program

This week is allotted for your thorough preparation for the Health Ministry Program that you will be conducting in your community. To guide you on how should this be done, read the following:

- Choose a target community that you want to benefit from your health ministry program.
- Focus on the goal and that is to motivate people to live better and longer. To achieve this aim, you need to **promote one healthy habit/behavior/practice and one spiritual component which is centered on God/Christ alone.**
- Choose the best and appropriate activities that you can use to achieve your goals. It could be a health fair, Sunday outreach, workshop, merry-go-round of topics, interactive circle of presentations, stations where you go by using a passport, etc. You may **choose the best activities that leave a better impact on the minds, feelings, and decision-making** of your audience.
- The health program will be **between 3 and 4 hours open to the public.**
- Create a way to evaluate that shows the impact of your program on your attendees (interview, testimonies, etc.)

These observations only underscore the importance of intentionality in integrating mission in online course design. Table 1.5 shows the observed intentionality of mission from teacher-generated course materials in the courses examined. Intentionality (★) is seen when the course overtly states its mission-related activities and results in the planned class activities, just like the following words in the Syllabus of course 7:

> "The students of this class will be exposed to different activities that will not only integrate theory into actual situation but also serve as an opportunity to do service to the community" (Course Outline, p. 1).

Table 1.5 Approaches to Mission Integration

Sources	Education				Public Health				Business	
	Course 1	Course 2	Course 3	Course 4	Course 5	Course 6	Course 7	Course 8	Course 9	Course 10
Devotional	★	★	★	★	★	★	★	★	✓	★
Forums	★	★	✓	✓	★	✓	✓	★	✓	✓
Content	✓	★	✓	-	★	-	-	-	-	-
Assignments	✓	★	-	✓	★	★	★	✓	✓	-
Syllabus	★	★	✓	★	★	★	★	★	-	✓

★Intentional integration ✓Incidental integration - No integration

If integration is not clear, yet produced outcomes that were mission-oriented, then it is marked 'incidental' (✓).

One interesting finding in the examination of intentionality of mission integration is its seeming relation to the Service approach. It appears that the courses that were mostly intentional (shaded in Table 1.5 above) in integrating mission were also the ones that engaged their students in actual mission activities (see Service approach in Table 1.4 above). This could mean that student engagement in actual mission work as a result of the class comes through intentional planning on the part of the teacher. It may be difficult to expect engagement without inclusion in the course plan.

The Mission Integration Model

Another interesting finding of this study is seen in the biblical basis of the resulting four approaches, which revealed behavioural outcomes that are important in mission integration (see Table 1.6). With the focus on Jesus as the model for acts of service, the natural outcome of worship is *submission* to His will (Matthew 6:10) to be able to do the same. As one gets closer to God, he/she begins to see things in God's eyes (Ephesians 1: 18-19), an *orientation* (worldview) that highlights mission in every field of study.

Table 1.6 Mission Integration Model

Approach	Outcome	Aspect
Worship	Submission (Matthew 6:10)	Spiritual
Cognitive/Worldview	Orientation (Ephesians 1: 18-19)	Mental
Character Formation	Resolution (1 Peter 4:19)	Emotional
Service	Action (Psalm 40:8)	Social

Furthermore, submission to God and the resulting change in orientation necessarily brings on commitment (1 Peter 4:19), a *resolution* to do His mission, which is the goal of character formation. These three outcomes lead a person to *action*—to engage in acts of service. Mission involvement then becomes a delight (Psalm 40:8) and not a burden.

What is remarkable about the outcomes of the four approaches to mission integration is their seeming connection to the four aspects of man—spiritual, mental, emotional, and social aspects. This is not to say, however, that the worldview approach is a mere mental activity and the service approach is mere socialization. The link is just observed since worldview entails a mental orientation to see things in God's perspectives, while service is done in relation to other people. This seeming linkage only shows that effective mission integration is akin to whole person development, which is the goal of Adventist education. The approaches are different yet all are equally important in integrating mission. This study then combines these four approaches and their outcomes to constitute the Mission Integration Model (Figure 1.3).

Figure 1.3 The mission integration model

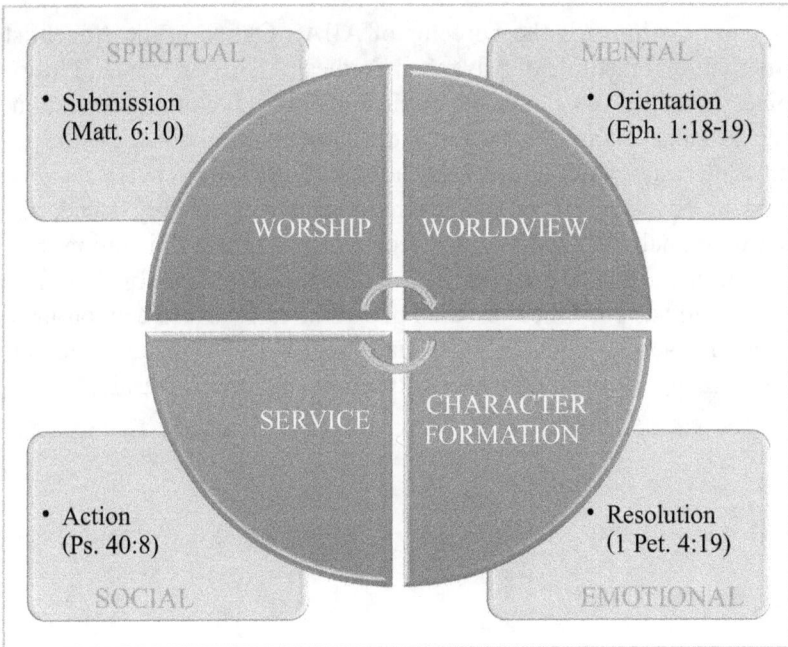

Conclusions and Recommendations

Mission integration in Adventist education is not just an option but a mandate. The nature of online learning, however, makes it challenging yet possible. As can be gleaned from the results of the documentary analyses, mission can be integrated in online courses using four approaches: worship, worldview, character formation, and service. Each is important for a complete mission integration.

The Mission Integration Model provides the total picture of a mission-oriented online course. It shows the approaches and the outcomes that need to be achieved for a holistic development of the students. Its strength is in highlighting the importance of active mission engagement in the course level.

This study, however, only looked into the existence of mission-oriented strategies in the courses reviewed. There is, therefore, a need for a study that deals with the impact of these strategies on online students. Likewise, the Mission Integration Model still needs to be validated in bigger populations. These areas can be the focus of future research.

Leni Casimiro

Leni Casimiro is the Director of AIIAS Online at the Adventist International Institute of Advanced Studies (AIIAS) in Cavite, Philippines. With her 16 years of experience in the field of online education, she has done extensive research in designing online courses, with specific interest on faith integration and mission-oriented course designs, student engagement, online teaching strategies, quality standards, learning analytics, instructional technology, and administration. She has been an invited speaker in both local and international conferences and has published research papers in various refereed journals. Leni also serves the AIIAS Graduate School as Associate Professor, specializing in curriculum and instruction, and online learning.

References

Anderson, S. (2009). How to kill Adventist education: And how to give it a fighting chance! Hagerstown, MD: Review and Herald.

Bowen, G. (2009). Document analysis as a qualitative research method. *Qualitative Research Journal, 9*(2), 27-40.

Blumschein, P. (2012). Intentional learning. In *Encyclopedia of the Sciences of Learning*, Norbert M. Seel (Ed.). US: Springer, p. 1600.

Casimiro, L. (2013). *Integration of faith and distance learning.* Paper presented at the 14th AIIAS International Conference on Business, Education, and Public Health. Adventist International institute of Advanced Studies, Cavite, Philippines, October 28-29, 2013.

du Preez, R. (2001). Integrating faith in the pre- post- and co-curricular practices of an Adventist campus. *Christ in the Classroom, 28*, 545-568. Retrieved from http://christintheclassroom.org/vol_28/ 28cc_545-568.htm

Eison, J. (2010). Using active learning instructional strategies to create excitement and enhance learning. *Jurnal Pendidikantentang Strategi Pembelajaran Aktif (Active Learning) Books, 2*(1), 1-10.

Fry, H., Ketteridge, S., & Marshall, S. (2009). *A handbook for teaching and learning in higher education* (3rd ed.). NY: Routledge.

Garrison, D., & Anderson, T. (2003). *E-learning in the 21st century.* London, England: RoutledgeFalmer.

General Conference Policy Manual (2003). Seventh-day Adventist philosophy of education. Education Department Policies, p. 1. Retrieved from http://circle.adventist.org/download/PhilStat2003.pdf

Hebert, A., & Hauf, P. (2015). Student learning through service learning: Effects on academic development, civic responsibility, interpersonal skills and practical skills. *Active Learning in Higher Education, 16*(1), 37-49.

Jung, J. (2015). *Character formation in online education.* Grand Rapids, MI: Zondervan.

Knight, G. (2017). The Great Commission and the educational imperative. *The Journal of Adventist Education, 79*(3), 4-10.

Kolb, D. (1984). *Experiential learning,* Englewood Cliffs, NJ: Prentice-Hall.

Payne, G., & Payne, J. (2004). *Key concepts in social research.* London, England: Sage.

Preisman, K. (2014). Teaching presence in online education: From the instructor's point-of-view. *Online Learning, 18*(3). Retrieved from https://olj.onlinelearningconsortium.org/index.php/olj/article/view/446

Ponyatovska, L. (2015). *Integration of faith and learning practices of faculty in the former Soviet country of Ukraine.* (Unpublished doctoral dissertation). Adventist International Institute of Advanced Studies, Cavite, Philippines.

Reese, H. W. (2011). The learning-by-doing principle. *Behavioral Development Bulletin. 17*(1), 1-19. doi: 10.1037/h0100597

Scott, J. (1990). A matter of record: Documentary sources in social research. Cambridge, MA: Polity Press.

Sheridan, K., & Kelly, M (2010). The indicators of instructor presence that are important to students in online courses. *MERLOT Journal of Online Learning and Teaching, 6*(4), pp.767-779.

Trye, A. (2017). An appreciative inquiry of the integration of faith and learning practices in Adventist higher educational institutions in Southeast Asia. (Unpublished doctoral dissertation). Adventist International Institute of Advanced Studies, Cavite, Philippines.

White, E. (2002). *Education.* Nampa, ID: Pacific Press.

White, E. (2011). *Counsels to parents, teachers, and students.* Nampa, ID: Pacific Press.

2. What Makes an Effective Online Course Facilitator in a Christian Institution

Safary Wa-Mbaleka. Associate Professor, Education Department.
Adventist International Institute of Advanced Studies, Silang, Philippines.
Corresponding Author: wa-mbalekas@aiias.edu

Abstract

Online education is now well established around the world. Adventists, although still not fully involved in it, have joined online education in a number of institutions. The resistance once held about online education decreases as the years go by. Although many guidelines have been published on what is expected from a good online course facilitator, it is also important to learn from online students what they believe makes the best online course facilitator, rather than to rely solely on pre-established sets of characteristics. This case study, based on an Adventist university in the Philippines that offers online programs, explored the viewpoint of online students through interviews to develop a list of characteristics that define an effective Christian online course facilitator. A taxonomy of seven indicators emerged. Effective Christian online facilitators demonstrate moral and Christian values, use effective online course facilitation strategies, give useful feedback, communicate effectively, use authentic assessments, plan well, and motivate students.

Introduction

The need for education is as old as human history. The human being was created to continually grow mentally (White, 2002). Sin, however, changed everything by pushing human beings in the opposite direction. Instead of continuously growing mentally, mental capacity continually decreased (Knight, 2010). Over the years, educators have tried to improve education for effectiveness and efficiency. With technological advances, the way people go about the business of delivering education has been transformed (Shelly, Gunter, & Gunter, 2010; Smaldino, Lowther, & Russell, 2012), although in many places around the world, embracing technology in education has been slow (Blin & Munro, 2008).

One of the major educational trends within the last decade has been the exponential increase in online course offerings (Allen & Seaman, 2008; Sun & Chen, 2016). In fact, universities with no online course offerings today are expected to struggle with student enrollment and finances (Wa-Mbaleka, 2013). With the rise of internet connectivity all around the world, online education continues to be on the rise. Unfortunately, while the focus is on technical knowledge, usually little emphasis is given on the training of faculty in online course design and delivery (Wa-Mbaleka, 2012, 2013), known technically as online instructional design and delivery (G. R. Morrison, Ross, Kalman, & Kemp, 2011). This trend is not uncommon in Christian higher education institutions (HEIs).

Three decades ago, Chickering and Gamson (1987) developed a list of seven best practices of good teaching at the undergraduate level. These included encouraging communication between educators and learners, promoting collaborative learning and active learning, providing prompt feedback, keeping students on task, communicating high expectations, and accommodating different learning styles. Although three decades old, this article still plays an important role in both face-to-face and online teaching today. Many of the principles for online teaching overlap with the seven principles from this article (see for instance, K. A. Morrison, 2011; Pelz, 2004; Stone & Perumean-Chaney, 2011; Strandberg & Campbell, 2014).

Teaching an online course, or rather, facilitating an online course, requires special skills that are different from face-to-face teaching, although there are areas of overlap. A few taxonomies or models have been published to list specific skills or strategies for online course facilitators. One of these is the TPACK Model, or technological pedagogical and content knowledge model by Mishra and Koehler (2006). Another is the list of 51 online course facilitation competencies by Smith (2005). Grant and Thornton (2007) developed a model for instructional design and delivery skills for undergraduate online course facilitators while DiPietro, Ferding, Black, and Preston (2008) proposed a model for K-12 online facilitators. Scarce, however, are models designed from the Christian perspective. This case study aimed to help address this specific gap, using data from an Adventist HEI located in the Philippines.

Literature Review

Since more and more educators have now understood that online course facilitation differs from face-to-face teaching, many have undertaken research and knowledge building on this important topic (see for instance, Bagdhadi, 2011; Baleni, 2015; DiPietro et al., 2008; Fish & Wickersham, 2009; Grant & Thornton, 2007; Kampov-Polevoi, 2010; Pelz, 2004; Poll, Widen, & Weller, 2014; Strandberg & Campbell, 2014; Thiede, 2012; Thomas, 2014; Wade & Wickersham, 2009). Most of the proposed lists of best practices for online course facilitation can be synthesized into five major relationships: relationship with facilitators themselves, relationship with students, relationship with the content, relationship with the technology, and relationship with the methods.

Facilitator's Relationship with Himself or Herself

Before anyone can facilitate an online course, they need understand who they are, why they wish to engage with online education, and what knowledge and skills they need in order to transition effectively to the online learning environment. It is true that no one is born an online course facilitator (Wa-Mbaleka, 2013). Many of the lists of best practices seem to favor a number of skills and values that are part of the facilitator's good relationship with himself or herself.

Online course facilitation requires facilitators to be caring, understanding, tolerant, patient, supportive, organized, and regularly accessible electronically (Dare, 2011; Poll et al., 2014; Stone & Perumean-Chaney, 2011; Tellent-Runnels et al., 2006), along with many other characteristics. Online students are separated from the course facilitator in time and place. Without a good relationship with self, the online course facilitator can discourage or frustrate the online learners. Showing he or she is ready, supportive of learners' academic growth, and available to them can create an atmosphere that facilitates online learning.

Online facilitators need to know why they wish to join online education. If they understand that the primary goal is to provide quality education and to make education more accessible to everyone and if they understand that the intention to democratize education (Giroux, 2004), they will approach online facilitation as an important mission. They will not join online education with misconceptions such as that online education is focused on making money, represents diploma mills, lacks teacher presence, and other misconceptions discussed in the literature over the years (see for instance, the discussions by Gahungu, Dereshiwsky, & Moan, 2006; Gambescia & Paolucci, 2009; and Sieber, 2005).

Online facilitators must know what skills they need to transition effectively and work well online. Most educators in face-to-face HEIs spent four years or more training in the field in which they teach. It is surprising that people who have never taken an online course nor taught online can be expected to rely only on common sense to suddenly become qualified to facilitate online courses. Any prospective online facilitator must go through training on practical online facilitation strategies (Bennet & Lockyer, 2004; Burke, 2005; Lim, 2003; Norris, 2008; Varvel Jr., 2007; Wa-Mbaleka, 2012). Rigorous training in online course facilitation can help increase the best online facilitation practices and consequently improve the online students' learning experience (Reinders, 2009).

Facilitator's Relationship with Students

The primary role of the online course facilitator is to be a guide on the side. Rather than teaching, the facilitator's predominant role is to guide the learners so that, through their personal exploration, they can achieve a meaningful online learning experience (Ashburn & Floden, 2006; Lofstrom & Nevgi, 2007). Meaningful learning is facilitated by having a knowledgeable, expert, supportive, motivating, inspiring, and effective travel guide—the facilitator. Online learners expect guidance, leadership, expertise, support, constructive and timely feedback, structure, and interaction from their facilitators (Poll et al., 2014). Online course facilitators are expected to focus on these factors to strengthen their relationship with their online students.

Facilitator's Relationship with the Content

In the TPACK Model, Mishra and Koehler (2006) emphasize the importance of the facilitator's content knowledge. It is one thing to know how to facilitate an online course; it is something else to know the content well that one is to facilitate (DiPietro et al., 2008). Expertise in the subject matter enables the online facilitator to focus attention on the other aspects of facilitation without having to devote time to learning the content to be facilitated. It is an imperative that online facilitators facilitate courses within their field of expertise. They must be knowledge experts.

Facilitator's Relationship with Technology

All online course management systems require technological skills from both the facilitators' and the learners' perspectives; being able to confront the technology from the learner's perspective is important. Therefore, the facilitator is required to know how to use technology to facilitate learning (Easton, 2003; Mishra & Koehler, 2006) as well to understand the technology with which the student engages as a learner. Everything in an online course depends on effective and efficient use of technology. Online course facilitators must be equipped with appropriate technological skills and enjoy using them to facilitate online learning. The facilitator needs to be competent with the technologies of both the teacher and the learner to truly support the learner.

Facilitator's Relationship with the Methods

Online facilitators cannot expect to teach the same way they taught in face-to-face settings. An abundance of literature exists on effective ways of facilitating online courses (see for instance, Bender, 2003; DiPietro et al., 2008; Easton, 2003; K. A. Morrison, 2011; Poll et al., 2014; Smith, 2005; Strandberg & Campbell, 2014). It is important for any HEI planning to train their prospective online course facilitators in online facilitation methods (Wa-Mbaleka, 2013). Prospective online course facilitators need to discover these strategies through personal reading and personal development strategies. A strong relationship with the facilitation methods that are effective for online settings can certainly assist in the quality and effectiveness of their online courses. Online facilitators must themselves remain active learners.

Research Questions

The main goal of this research study was to develop a practical taxonomy synthesizing the qualities of an effective online course facilitator in a Christian setting. The focus of this study was specifically on the following research questions:

1. What are the qualities of an effective online course facilitator in a Christian higher education institution?
2. What characteristics are specific to an effective Christian online course facilitator?

Methodology

This case study explored the qualities that students at a private Adventist HEI in the Philippines expected of a Christian online course facilitator. While a number of taxonomies have been developed about qualities of a good online course facilitator, few, if any, of those are focused specifically on Christian HEIs. In this methodology section, the discussion includes the research design, setting, sampling, data collection, data analysis, ethical considerations, and my personal reflexivity, as this is a qualitative research study.

Research Design

For purposes of this study, a qualitative case study design was selected. Case study is preferred when variables may not be well known, or the phenomenon and the context are intertwined (Stake, 2010; Yin, 2014, 2015). It is also appropriate when the focus is about a process, an event, a program, an institution, or an individual (Baxter & Jack, 2008; Creswell, 2013; Creswell & Poth, 2016; Merriam, 2009; Merriam & Tisdell, 2015). In this case, although the study included 24 students from one institution, it is about the way they all viewed this topic. In fact, trying to find the best practices of effective online course facilitators was from the perspective of the selected HEI since all the students attended the same institution. Therefore, it is a single case study, with this HEI as the unit of analysis. Most likely what transpired from the best practices of the effective online course facilitators reflects the values of the selected HEI.

Research Setting

This case study was conducted at an Adventist HEI located in the Philippines. The institution offers graduate programs in business, education, health, and theological fields, both at the master's and doctoral levels. This HEI is based solidly on the philosophy of Seventh-day Adventist education, with the goal being to train exemplary Christian leaders fit to work anywhere in the world. The institution has a higher number of foreign faculty and students than local ones. Probably, Christian values and affordability are parts of the attraction of foreign students to this university. It offers face-to-face courses mainly, but also offers a few online programs and several online subjects. The division of online learning had been running for 11 years at the time this study was conducted.

Sampling

This study used purposive sampling, involving three groups, with a total of 24 students. The first group of nine students (referred to here as Team A) were mainly master's students who had previously taken at least one online course at this HEI. The second group of 10 doctoral students (referred to here as Team B) who had previously taken the e-Learning course as a hybrid course, had experienced taking at least one online course, and had designed at least one online course as a course requirement. The third group included five doctoral students (referred to here as Team C) who had also completed the e-Learning course but did not participate in the preliminary data collection of Team A or B. They played the role of peer reviewers after the preliminary data analysis.

In Team A, students were recruited only if they had taken at least one online course. Although recruitment was open to all, only nine participated. In Team B, all students from one of the e-Learning doctoral courses participated. In Team C, only five were selected because they too had taken the e-Learning course from a more recent year, had performed exceptionally well when they took the e-Learning course, and they did not participate in the data collection as did Teams A and B.

Data Collection

One of the preferred methods of data collection in qualitative research is interviews (Corbin & Strauss, 2015; Creswell & Poth, 2016; Crowe et al., 2011; Yin, 2014). In this study, both oral and written interviews were used. Data collection included three major phases. In the first phase, 10 students in the e-Learning course (Team B) participated in a class activity where they were required to develop a list of the best practices of effective online course facilitators in a Christian instructional setting. This oral interview was done as a class activity. This data was authentic, given that their attention was not on a possible research project, but rather on learning in face-to-face class discussion.

In the second phase, students who had taken at least one online course were contacted through the institution's division of online learning. They received an email requesting them to indicate seven qualities of effective online course facilitators. An online written interview was sent to them subsequently asking them to identify the seven best qualities of effective online facilitators and explain why each quality was important. Team A is the only group that was involved in this written interview.

After the data from the first two phases was compiled, analyzed, compared, and contrasted, it was synthesized into one table. The table was sent to Team C for their comments. This team served as peer reviewers and proposed a few minor changes. The final table presented in the results reflects the synthesis of the data from the three phrases and three groups.

Data Analysis

Data analysis involved thematic analysis, as discussed in the literature (Miles, Huberman, & Saldaña, 2014; Saldaña, 2011). The thematic analysis led to the final seven major characteristics of an effective Christian online course facilitator. The thematic analysis was verified by Team C of the research participants for the purposes of peer review.

Ethical Considerations

This study was conducted as a service to the university's division of online learning's continuous improvement goal and in line with the university's research ethics standards. It followed ethical research practices consistent with those defined by Lune & Berg (2017), Taylor, Bogdan, & DeVault (2016), Thorne (2016), and Wa-Mbaleka (2017). Participants were informed that their participation was voluntary and their names would be kept confidential. Additionally, the findings are reported in aggregated form to assure that individual participants cannot be identified.

Researcher's Reflexivity

In qualitative research, it is important to acknowledge our bias (Lichtman, 2013; Wa-Mbaleka, 2017). This research may have been influenced by some of my past personal academic and professional experiences. Given that I completed my doctoral program online, within the field of online instructional design, I have been exposed to a plethora of characteristics of good online course facilitation. Additionally, I have designed and facilitated online courses for more than a decade. Lastly, I engage in the teaching activity as a Christian online course facilitator. All these factors had the potential to influence the data collection and data analysis. It was for this reason that Team

C conducted a peer review to identify any evident bias I may have bought to the analysis of the material.

Results

This study explored what students who had taken at least one online course at the selected HEI thought were the qualities of effective Christian online course facilitators. Three different types of participants participated in the study. Data from the online written interview was simply downloaded and coded in a Word document. Data from the class activity was also coded. The analysis from the online group yielded five primary themes. When the data from the face-to-face group was analyzed, the list increased to seven themes, which is the final number of the themes of this study. A table was created to compare and contrast the data from the online group and the face-to-face group. Later, a new table was created that combined the data from both groups. This new table was sent to the five participants who played the role of the peer reviewers. Table 1 synthesizes the major findings of this study.

Table 2.1 A Taxonomy of Indicators of an Effective Christian Online Course Facilitator

Major Indicators	Specific Indicators
1. Demonstrates moral and Christian values	a. Is friendly
	b. Is non-judgmental
	c. Is godly
	d. Is compassionate and supportive
	e. Integrates faith and learning in devotionals and throughout the course
	f. Prays with and for the students
	g. Gives a second chance on assignments
2. Uses effective online course facilitation strategies	a. Is a good role model
	b. Monitors the class regularly
	c. Facilitates course from first to last module
	d. Focuses on higher order thinking
	e. Sets a positive tone
	f. Uses a variety of methods
	g. Provides guidance and leadership

Major Indicators	Specific Indicators
3. Gives useful feedback	a. Gives quality feedback: clear, timely, honest, constructive
	b. Gives feedback on each course requirement
	c. Acknowledges students' special effort in class
	d. Grades fairly
	e. Gives personalized feedback
	f. Gives clear feedback for continuous improvement
	g. Reacts to students' postings
	h. Focuses on the mastery of the content
4. Communicates effectively	a. Encourages students
	b. Is open
	c. Sends both personal and class messages
	d. Informs students when traveling or when unavailable
	e. Shows availability when he/she is needed
	f. Deals effectively with inflammatory messages
5. Uses authentic assessments	a. Provides clear instructions for every requirement
	b. Asks open-ended questions
	c. Discourages copy-paste answers
	d. Is honest
	e. Diversifies assignments
	f. Creates original quizzes
6. Plans well	a. Is well prepared
	b. Checks online links to quality articles/readings
	c. Schedules and uses live virtual meetings
	d. Sets enough time for quizzes
	e. Structures well all class instructions and activities
	f. Prepares and uses clear grading rubrics
	g. Anticipates the needs of the students
	h. Has useful syllabus with clear assignment instructions
	i. Considers different student needs and learning preferences
7. Motivates students	a. Encourages creative and critical thinking
	b. Is understanding
	c. Extends deadlines when necessary
	d. Believes in students' capability and lets them know
	e. Includes class participation in grade
	f. Sends students personalized private messages
	g. Integrates the affective domain in facilitation
	h. Keeps instructions sweet, simple, and structured (KISSS)
	i. Promotes a safe learning environment
	j. Uses debatable topics to engage less active students
	k. Promotes learners' peer review

This study yielded a taxonomy of seven traits of effective Christian online course facilitators. From the most recurring to the least recurring, the seven themes are presented here. According to the participants, an effective Christian online course facilitator demonstrates moral and Christian values, uses effective online course facilitation strategies, gives useful feedback, communicates effectively, uses authentic assessments, plans well, and motivates students.

Indicator 1: The Facilitator Demonstrates Moral and Christian Values

It is no surprise that demonstrating moral and Christian values was the most recurring theme in this Adventist educational setting. After all, it is quite difficult to imagine Christian education being facilitated by non-Christian facilitators. It is an oxymoron, whether it happens or not. From this study, it became clear that eight specific expectations are important for a Christian online facilitator.

The online facilitator is expected to be friendly, non-judgmental, godly, compassionate, and supportive. All these characteristics are a clear revelation of the demonstration of God's love, as summarized in the love of the neighbor (Mark 12:31) and the Golden Rule (Mat. 7:12). In a nutshell, a facilitator in an online setting demonstrates and upholds moral and Christian values. The actions of a Christian educator must reflect moral and Christian values because integration of faith and learning cannot be decorative only; it must also be demonstrated in the life and actions of the educator (J. W. Taylor, 2012). As one participant stated, "The facilitator must reflect the love, grace, and understanding Jesus showed to everyone." Christian values must permeate all aspects of the Christian online education (Wa-Mbaleka, 2013).

In this study, the actions of a Christian facilitator included praying with and for his or her students, integration of faith and learning in the online devotionals and throughout the course, and provision of an assessment structure that allows students to utilize feedback in subsequent assessments, effectively providing a second chance by addressing their errors in an assignment when an earlier phase of the assessment identified aspects which did not meet the expectations. The use of progressive assessment strategies is important in this. A Christian facilitator must be a man or woman of prayer and must integrate faith and learning into the content and in the content delivery.

After all, the work of education and redemption are believed to be one (White, 2002). A Christian educator facilitating an online course in a Christian institution must therefore embrace and demonstrate Christian values.

Indicator 2: The Facilitator Uses Effective Online Course Facilitation Strategies

The literature is full of many online course facilitation competencies (see for instance, Bender, 2003; DiPietro et al., 2008; Grant & Thornton, 2007; K. A. Morrison, 2011; Orr & Williams, 2009; Pelz, 2004; Strandberg & Campbell, 2014). Of all of them, six were emphasized in this study. An effective facilitator must be a good role model and monitor the class regularly. He or she is visible by making postings regularly. In an 8-12-week online course (which is the common practice for online courses), logging on in the course four to five times a week may be ideal. When students post questions in the course, they should not have to wait for days before an answer is posted. The same applies to emails, which should be addressed within 24 hours under normal circumstances. On the same note, effective facilitators are present from the beginning to the end of the term of the course, without skipping any module. One participant emphasized the reality that "students can trace the last time the professor logged in;" and this is true with many different course management systems. In all these activities, the facilitator is expected to focus on higher thinking skills. Focusing on higher order thinking skills is especially important for higher education.

Effective facilitators set a positive tone from the very beginning of the course. The recommended strategies in this study include the facilitator's self-introduction and a requirement for students to introduce themselves. This practice helps students know their facilitator as well as each other well. Facilitators must find ways to build a community of learners. At the beginning of the course, they should use some ice-breakers to make the students comfortable. Last, they set a good example in interacting with students so that students can emulate them.

Effective facilitators use a variety of facilitation methods. Those proposed in this study include usage of a good sense of humor, creativity in new facilitation methods, provision of new ideas to students, effective use of technology to enhance the learning experience, and integration of videoconferencing in online course facilitation. Just as with all other learners, online learners have different learning preferences. Diversity in methods of facilitation can cater to the different needs of learners.

Effective facilitators provide guidance and leadership in the online course, through supporting struggling students without discrimination. They focus more on facilitating than instructing. Lectures, when used, should not be lengthy. At the selected university, video lectures are kept to the maximum length of 12 minutes each. They are used either to explain a difficult concept or to introduce a course module. Effective facilitators also promote effective collaboration among students. One participant emphasized that facilitators should "create a sense of community in the online world among the students." Additionally, they should have regular online office hours to guide students who may be in need of synchronous orientation.

Indicator 3: The Facilitator Gives Useful Feedback

In the online learning environment, potentially there is a greater need for feedback than in face-to-face classes; online students rely heavily on quality feedback. Quality feedback must be clear, timely, honest, and constructive, according to the participants of this study. Such feedback must be given on each and every course requirement. Feedback that does not meet the criteria listed here may not have the expected formative impact on the learning experience of the online students.

Additionally, effective facilitators use other important and practical strategies to give useful feedback. They acknowledge students' special efforts in the online class, such as posting an announcement about special accomplishments of some students, without revealing their grades, of course. They grade fairly and personalize the feedback. They give clear feedback that allows for learners' continuous improvement. They must respond to students' postings; these reactions give evidence that the facilitator has indeed read the student postings. Feedback focuses on helping students master the content of the course.

Indicator 4: The Facilitator Communicates Effectively

Based on the results of this study, effective communication in online instruction involves six important methods. Effective facilitators are encouragers; their communication focuses on encouraging rather than scaring, discouraging, or demoralizing online learners. Effective facilitators are available to students when students need them. That includes checking emails regularly. Effective facilitators are open and straightforward in their communication. They send both personal and class messages as the need arises. If traveling or away for any reason, they inform students ahead of time.

Effective facilitators show availability when students need them. When students contact a facilitator, they are most likely already frustrated. All they need at that moment is a timely reply from the facilitator with a concise answer. Delayed replies to messages simply send a message to the students that the facilitator is not available to support them. Repeated delay in these replies can easily lead online students to lose their motivation and eventually lead to dropout either from the course or even the whole online program.

Effective facilitators deal effectively with inappropriate messages posted by students. Issues may arise in an online course at any time where there is the potential for inappropriate messages, which may be demeaning to others, to be posted on discussion boards by students. In this study, participants recommended several practical steps facilitators can use to deal with inflammatory messages. They need to set appropriate ground rules for the use of notice boards. They should not ignore inflammatory messages, as these can quickly get out of hand; they cannot just hope that the problem will simply fade away. They should discourage inflammatory messages once they happen. They should show empathy to the victim of such messages while helping the offender to prevent recurrence. Institutions must develop appropriate policies which will provide a framework for students to work in the online environment in harmony. This is a good opportunity to discuss the concept of respect for others when working in such an environment.

Indicator 5: The Facilitator Uses Authentic Assessments

Effectively assessing online students is one of the controversial issues many people complain about (Rowe, 2004). A number of educators see the potential for cheating to be much easier online than it is in face-to-face classes. For this reason, participants in this study recommended use of authentic assessments. Six strategies were specifically recommended.

1. Provide clear instructions for every course requiremen. These instructions must be clear and complete. Presenting instructions in a bulleted form or in lists will guide learners

better than using long paragraphs (Wa-Mbaleka, 2012). This approach lowers the learners' cognitive load, thus, motivating learners even more.

2. Give preference to open-ended questions rather than multiple-choice questions as the latter can easily lead to cheating.

3. Discourage copy-and-paste kinds of responses as a means of answering questions; a culture of honesty needs to be fostered.

4. A diversity of assignments needs to be used so that there are multiple ways for students to demonstrate their mastery of the content.

5. When quizzes are used, they must be original quizzes, not quizzes that are accessible online or in books. Ideally, quizzes should be used primarily to practice new concepts, where the quiz can assist students' understanding of important information and concepts.

Indicator 6: The Facilitator Plans Well

Effective facilitators, in the way they manage their online courses, demonstrate whether they are well prepared prior to the beginning of the course. For instance, a course with an outdated course syllabus and dead links to instructional materials can easily send a strong negative message that a course facilitator was not prepared. Therefore, facilitators must check every link to class articles or readings before the first day of the class to make sure they are active. They must also update everything that needs updating before the first day of class.

Effective facilitators schedule and use live meetings. These meetings should not be scheduled as the need arises, rather they must be pre-planned so that students know that they need to be a part of the course through participating in these discussions. They also make sure that all class instructions and activities are well structured; structure referring to having clear guidelines, a logical sequence of instructions, different learning activities, and enough time allotted to complete each activity.

For performance-based assessments, facilitators must ensure that each assessment task has an associated grading rubric. Rubrics help students know what is expected for each assignment and how many points are allotted for each component of the assignment (Wa-Mbaleka, 2012). Using rubrics can avoid several complaints and misunderstandings related to subjective grading of non-objective assessments. Facilitators anticipate the needs of their students; they create both the assignment instructions and grading rubrics to facilitate students' engagement in course components. They make sure all course requirements have clearly defined deadlines and "signposting."

Lastly, effective facilitators plan different content delivery formats to cater to the needs of the different learning styles and multiple intelligences. While this recommendation probably fits best for the online instructional design phase than for online instructional delivery, the reality is that it came up in the data and thus is something that the course facilitator must consider before the course begins. Online students, as with all students, learn differently; therefore, content should be delivered according to their need for diversity of learning approaches.

Indicator 7: The Facilitator Motivates Students

The last indicator that came from the data related to motivation of students. Because they do not usually get the chance to interact face-to-face with the facilitator or other students, online learners need to receive encouragement from their facilitators. This study revealed 11 different ways of motivating online learners. Effective facilitators encourage students in creative and critical thinking. This focus takes learners beyond the ordinary and the obvious. Effective facilitators are understanding. They accommodate students when special needs arise. Sometimes, they extend deadlines when it is necessary to help students learn better. One participant stated there is a need to support online students, "…..especially for first-time students working and studying at the same time; the work can get overwhelming; it helps to know you have some sort of support system and direction to motivate you to keep going and not to give up". This demonstration of *humanity* creates an environment where interest in the learners' success is held in high regard. This approach should be done in such away as not to be confused with a laissez-faire environment.

Additionally, effective facilitators believe in their students' capability and let those learners know about it. Guiding learners with such a positive attitude can help learners perform to their best ability. Effective facilitators also include class participation (through online postings) in the grading system. This practice makes it possible for learners to participate in the class discussions. Another way effective facilitators motivate their students is to send private, personalized messages to them. Such a practice demonstrates that the facilitator cares for each individual student; not just the class in general.

There were four other strategies proposed in this study to motivate online learners. Firstly, integration of the affective domain in the instructional delivery; this makes online learners feel that someone does truly care for them. Second, they use the KISSS model, where they Keep Instructions Sweet (attractive), Simple, and Structured. When instructions are presented in this way, students are motivated to read and follow them. Next, it is important to promote a safe learning environment, where students feel free to contribute to the learning of everyone. Effective facilitators promote trust in their online courses. They also use debatable topics to engage less-engaged students in addition to many other strategies mentioned in the literature (see for instance, those by Dixson, 2010). Effective facilitators promote learners' peer review. When online learners peer review each other's work before submission, the quality of their work can be improved and thus yield a better learning outcome.

Conclusion

This case study conducted at a Christian HEI in the Philippines yielded a taxonomy of seven indicators of what effective Christian online facilitators do. They demonstrate what effective facilitation is, but in an environment that is supportive of moral and Christian values: they use effective online course facilitation strategies, they give useful feedback, they communicate effectively, they use authentic assessments, they plan well, and they motivate their students in the learning process. Demonstrating moral and Christian values was a specific element that came out strongly in this study as opposed to much of the existing literature. For the purpose of improving the quality of online education at the selected HEI, all faculty there must be exposed to this taxonomy and the strategies it promotes. The strategies proposed in this paper have relevance to other similar HEIs and the potential for their use must be considered by the reader (Bogdan and Biklen, 2007).

Faculty who are confronting online learning, especially those for doing so for the first time, need to be provided with staff development promoting the seven indicators. Training must be given on the comprehensive aspects and strategies of integrating faith and learning. Faculty must also learn the practical principles of designing and delivering effective online courses which espouse the strategies presented here.

Finally there is a need for further research to continue improving this taxonomy. A quantitative study that uses the content of this taxonomy should be carried out with a large population to make a more refined taxonomy. Such a study will be much more easily replicable in different Christian online instructional settings. Additionally, the seven indicators could be studied by exploring each of them in more depth. Last, more research in Christian online education is needed from different parts of the world to increase this wealth of knowledge.

Safary Wa-Mbaleka

Safary Wa-Mbaleka is an associate professor of in the education department at Adventist International Institute of Advanced Studies (AIIAS), Philippines. He teaches e-learning, education courses, applied linguistics courses, and research courses. In addition to obtaining a doctoral degree in online education, he has taught and designed online courses for more than 10 years in a number of American universities.

References

Allen, I. E., & Seaman, J. (2008). *Staying the course: Online education in the United States.* Retrieved from http://sloanconsortium.org/publications/survey/staying_course

Ashburn, E. A., & Floden, R. E. (Eds.). (2006). *Meaningful learning using technology.* New York, NY: Teachers College.

Bagdhadi, Z. D. (2011). Best practices in online education: Online instructors, courses, and administrators. *Turkish Online Journal of Distance Education, 12*(3), 109-117. Retrieved from http://files.eric.ed.gov/fulltext/EJ965061.pdf

Baleni, Z. G. (2015). Online formative assessment in higher education: Its pros and cons. *The Electronic Journal of e-Learning, 13*(4), 228-236. Retrieved from http://issuu.com/academic-conferences.org/docs/ejel-volume13-issue4-article433?mode=a_p

Baxter, P., & Jack, S. (2008). Qualitative case study methodology: Study design and implementation for novice researchers. *The Qualitative Report, 13*(4), 544-559. Retrieved from http://www.nova.edu/ ssss/QR/QR13-4/baxter.pdf

Bender, T. (2003). *Discussion-based online teaching to enhance student learning: Theory, practice and assessment.* Sterling, VA: Stylus.

Bennet, S., & Lockyer, L. (2004). Becoming an online teacher: Adapting to a changed environment for teaching and learning in higher education. *Educational Medial International, 41*(3), 231-244.

Blin, F., & Munro, M. (2008). Why hasn't technology disrupted academics' teaching practices? Understanding resistance to change through the lenses of activity theory. *Computers & Education, 50*, 475-490.

Bogdan, R. C., & Biklen, S. K. (2007). *Qualitative research for education: An introduction to theories and methods* (5th ed.). New York, NY: Ally and Bacon.

Burke, L. A. (2005). Transitioning to online course offerings: Tactical and strategic considerations. *Journal of Interactive Online Learning, 4*(2), 94-107.

Chickering, A. W., & Gamson, Z. F. (1987). Seven principles for good practice in undergraduate education. *AAHE Bulletin, 3*, 2-7. Retrieved from https://files.eric.ed.gov/fulltext/ED282491.pdf

Corbin, J., & Strauss, A. (2015). *Basics of qualitative research: Techniques and procedures for developing grounded theory* (4th ed.). Los Angeles, CA: Sage.

Creswell, J. W. (2013). *Qualitative inquiry and research design: Choosing among five approaches* (3rd ed.). Thousand Oaks, CA: Sage.

Creswell, J. W., & Poth, C. N. (2016). *Qualitative inquiry and research design: Choosing among five approaches* (4th ed.). Thousand Oaks, CA: Sage.

Crowe, S., Creswell, K., Robertson, A., Huby, G., Avery, A., & Sheikeh, A. (2011). The case study approach. *Medical Research Methodology, 11*, 100-108. Retrieved from http://www.biomedcentral.com/1471-2288/11/100

Dare, A. (2011). (Dis)embodied difference in the online class: Vulnerability, visibility, and social justice. *MERLOT Journal of Online Learning and Teaching, 7*(2), 279-287. Retrieved from http://jolt.merlot.org/vol7no2/dare_0611.pdf

DiPietro, M., Ferding, R. E., Black, E. W., & Preston, M. (2008). Best practices in teaching K-12 online: Lessons learnt from Michigan Virtual Schools teachers. *Journal of Interactive Online Learning, 7*(1), 10-35. Retrieved from http://www.ncolr.org/jiol/issues/pdf/7.1.2.pdf

Dixson, M. D. (2010). Creating effective student engagement in online courses: What do students find engaging? *Journal of the scholarship of teaching and learning, 10*(2), 1-13. Retrieved from https://www.iupui.edu/~josotl/archive/vol_10/no_2/v10n2dixson.pdf

Easton, S. S. (2003). Clarifying the instructor's role in online distance learning. *Communication Education, 52*(2), 87-105.

Fish, W. W., & Wickersham, L. E. (2009). Best practices for online instructors: Reminders. *The Quarterly Review of Distance Education, 10*(3), 279-284.

Gahungu, A., Dereshiwsky, M., & Moan, E. (2006). Finally I can be with my students 24/7, individually and in group: A survey of faculty teaching online. *Journal of Interactive Online Learning, 5*(2), 118-142.

Gambescia, S. F., & Paolucci, R. (2009). Academic fidelity and integrity as attributes of university online degree program offerings. *Online Journal of Distance Learning Administration, 12*(1).

Giroux, H. A. (2004). Critical pedagogy and the postmodern/modern divide: Towards a pedagogy of democratization. *Teacher Education Quarterly, 31*(1), 31-47.

Grant, M. R., & Thornton, H. R. (2007). Best practices in undergraduate adult-centered online learning: Mechanisms for course design and delivery. *MERLOT Journal of Online Learning and Teaching, 3*(4), 346-356. Retrieved from http://jolt.merlot.org/documents/grant.pdf

Kampov-Polevoi, J. (2010). Considerations for supporting faculty in transitioning a course to online format. *Online Journal of Distance Learning Administration, 13*(2).

Knight, G. R. (2010). Redemptive education, part 1: A philosophical foundation. *The Journal of Adventist Education, 73*(1), 4-21. Retrieved from http://circle.adventist.org/files/jae/en/jae201073010418.pdf

Lichtman, M. (2013). *Qualitative research in education: A user's guide* (3rd ed.). Thousand Oaks, CA: Sage.

Lim, J. (2003). Essentials: Structure and routine in online courses. *The Journal of Adventist Education, 65*(5), 16-31. Retrieved from http://circle.adventist.org/files/jae/en/jae200365041601.pdf

Lofstrom, E., & Nevgi, A. (2007). From strategic planning to meaningful learning: Diverse perspectives on the development of web-based teaching and learning in higher education. *British Journal of Educational Technology, 38*(2), 312-324.

Lune, H., & Berg, B. L. (2017). *Qualitative research methods for the social sciences* (9th ed.). New York, NY: Pearson.

Merriam, S. B. (2009). *Qualitative research: A guide to design and implementation.* San Francisco, CA: John Wiley & Sons.

Merriam, S. B., & Tisdell, E. J. (2015). *Qualitative research: A guide to design and implementation.* New York, NY: John Wiley & Sons.

Miles, M. B., Huberman, A. M., & Saldaña, J. (2014). *Qualitative data analysis: A methods sourcebook.* Los Angeles, CA: Sage.

Mishra, P., & Koehler, M. J. (2006). Technological pedagogical content knowledge: A framework for integrating technology in teacher knowledge. *Teachers College Record, 108*(6), 1017-1054.

Morrison, G. R., Ross, S. M., Kalman, H. K., & Kemp, J. E. (2011). *Designing effective instruction* (6th ed.). New York, NY: Wiley.

Morrison, K. A. (2011). Synchronous online teaching: Using web-conferencing tools for discussion and activity-rich courses. *International Journal of Instructional Technology and Distance Learning, 8*(12), 19-32. Retrieved from http://www.itdl.org/Journal/Dec_11/Dec_11.pdf

Norris, K. Z. (2008). Online teacher professional development: Knowledge construction and knowledge transfer. (doctoral dissertation), Capella University, Minneapolis.

Orr, R., & Williams, M. R. (2009). Institutional efforts to support faculty in online teaching. *Innovative Higher Education, 34*(4), 257-268.

Pelz, B. (2004). (My) Three principles of effective online pedagogy. *JALN, 8*(3), 33-46. Retrieved from http://files.eric.ed.gov/fulltext/EJ909855.pdf

Poll, K., Widen, J., & Weller, S. (2014). Six instructional best practices for online engagement and retention. *Journal of Online Doctoral Education, 1*(1), 57-72.

Reinders, H. (2009). Teaching (with) technology: The scope and practice of teacher education for technology. *Prospect: An Australian journal of TESO, 24*(3), 15-23. Retrieved from http://www.ameprc.mq.edu.au/docs/prospect_journal/volume_24_no_3/Reinders.pdf

Rowe, N. C. (2004). Cheating in online student assessment: Beyond plagiarism. *Online Journal of Distance Learning Administration, 7*(2). Retrieved from http://www.westga.edu/~distance/ojdla/summer72/rowe72.html

Saldaña, J. (2011). *Fundamentals of qualitative research.* Oxford, MA: Oxford University Press.

Shelly, G. B., Gunter, G. A., & Gunter, R. (2010). *Teachers discovering computers: Integrating technology and digital media in the classroom* (6th ed.). Boston, MA: Cengage Learning.

Sieber, J. E. (2005). Misconceptions and realities about teaching online. *Science and Engineering Ethics, 11*, 329-340.

Smaldino, S. E., Lowther, D. L., & Russell, J. W. (2012). *Instructional technology and media for learning* (10th ed.). Boston, MA: Allyn & Bacon.

Smith, T. C. (2005). Fifty-one competencies for online instruction. *Journal of Educators Online, 2*(2), 1-18.

Stake, R. E. (2010). *Qualitative research: Studying how things work.* New York: NY: The Guilford Press.

Stone, M. T., & Perumean-Chaney, S. (2011). The benefits of online teaching for traditional classroom pedagogy: A case study for improving face-to-face instruction. *MERLOT Journal of Online Learning and Teaching and Learning, 7*(3). Retrieved from http://jolt.merlot.org/vol7no3/stone_0911.htm

Strandberg, A. G., & Campbell, C. (2014). Online teaching best practices to better engage students with quantitative material. *Journal of instructional Pedagogies, 15*, 1-14. Retrieved from https://eric.ed.gov/?id=EJ1106761

Sun, A., & Chen, X. (2016). Online education and its effective practice: A research review. *Journal of Information and Technology Education: Research, 15*, 157-190.

Taylor, J. W. (2012). A biblical foundation for integrating faith and learning. *The Journal of Adventist Education, Summer*, 8-14. Retrieved from http://circle.adventist.org/files/jae/en/jae201274050807.pdf

Taylor, S. J., Bogdan, R. C., & DeVault, M. (2016). *Introduction to qualitative research methods: A guidebook and resource* (4th ed.). New York, NY: John Wiley & Sons.

Tellent-Runnels, M. K., Thomas, J. A., Lan, W. Y., Cooper, S., Ahern, T. C., Shaw, S. M., & Liu, X. (2006). Teaching courses online: A review of the research. *Review of Educational Research, 76*(1), 93-135.

Thiede, R. (2012). Best practices with online courses. *US-China Education Review, A*(2), 135-141.

Thomas, W. (2014). Parallel universes: Student and teacher expectations and interactions in online vs face-to-face teaching and learning environments. *Ergo, 3*(3), 37-48. Retrieved from https://www.ojs.unisa.edu.au/index.php/ergo/article/view/908/769

Thorne, S. (2016). *Interpretive description: Qualitative research for applied practice* (2nd ed.). New York, NY: Routledge.

Varvel Jr., V. E. (2007). Master online teacher competencies. *Online Journal of Distance Learning Administration, 10*(1), Online version. Retrieved from http://www.westga.edu/~distance/ojdla/spring101/varvel101.htm

Wa-Mbaleka, S. (2012). Designing learning modules for online courses: The 5-WH approach. *International Forum, 15*(2), 29-41. Retrieved from http://internationalforum.aiias.edu/images/vol15no02/infojournal-vol15no2_wa-mbaleka.pdf

Wa-Mbaleka, S. (2013). Instructional design foundations of online education. *International Forum, 16*(1), 49-61. Retrieved from http://internationalforum.aiias.edu/images/vol16no01/article4-wa-mbaleka.pdf

Wa-Mbaleka, S. (2017). Fostering quality in qualitative research: A list of practical strategies. *International Forum, 20*(1), 58-80.

Wade, W. F., & Wickersham, L. E. (2009). Best practices for online isntructors: Reminders. *The Quarterly Review of Distance Education, 10*(3), 279-284.

White, E. G. (2002). *Education*. Nampa, ID: Pacific Press.

Yin, R. K. (2014). *Case study research: Design and methods* (7th ed.). Newbury Park, CA: SAGE.

Yin, R. K. (2015). *Qualitative research from start to finish* (2nd ed.). New York, NY: Guilford Publications.

Empowerment

Creating online education strategies to empower and enable students, staff, and faculty is an essential aspect of designing quality online education delivery. In this section, Glynis Bradfield examines the effects of proactive and appreciative advising practices on online student persistence. Maria Northcote, Anthony Williams, Kevin Petrie, John Seddon, and Sherene Hattingh document the process of developing faculty training and support resources. Anthony Williams, Maria Northcote, and John Reddin explain the Virtual Mentoring Program (VMP) and the Learning Engagement Analytics Platform (LEAP) which are methods to increase persistence and retention. Finally, Anthony Williams and Maria Northcote report on the results of using research to develop a center for teaching, learning and scholarship, focusing on the support of online and web-enhanced education.

3. Advising Strategies that Increase Online Student Persistence

Glynis Bradfield. Director of Distance Student Services. Andrews University, Berrien Springs, United States. Corresponding Author: glynisb@andrews.edu

Abstract

Research indicates that a crucial factor to student persistence is the quality of the student's relationship with at least one person in the university community, often the academic advisor or supervisor. Even though persistence rates are consistently lower for online and non-traditional (mature) students than traditional (young adult) students on residential campuses, online education continues to grow. This mixed methods study reflects one university's journey to build capacity and quality of student services for those studying online. Considering academic advisor evaluation survey data, online learning management and student information system quantitative data, along with online student interview qualitative data, this action research indicates that proactive and appreciative advising practices impact persistence and degree completion for globally-distributed students studying online.

Introduction

Numerous factors contribute to the persistence of students studying online. A complex array of personal characteristics (Harrell & Bower, 2011), such as the student's prior knowledge and skill sets; preferred learning style; social life; family and work responsibilities; mental, emotional and spiritual health; impact motivation and self-efficacy, and persistence to graduation. Course characteristics (Hershkovitz & Nachmias, 2011), including instructor presence, quality of feedback, ease of use, delivery mode, and types of instructional media contribute significantly to student success.

Many universities report course retention (i.e. persistence from year to year) rates eight or more percentage points lower for online courses compared to on-campus courses across the United States (Kena et al., 2014; Knapp, Kelly-Reid, & Ginder, 2012; Lokken & Mullins, 2014; Ross et al., 2012). Similarly lower rates are reported in other countries (Carnoy, Rabling, Castano-Munoz, Duart Monto-liu, & Sancho-Vinuesa, 2012; Schneller & Holmberg, 2014a). Nota-bly, on-campus undergraduate retention rates reflect predominantly traditional students studying full-time, where online retention rates reflect a wider pool of predominantly post-traditional students who are studying part-time, with work, family, and community responsi-bilities vying for their attention. While differences in student popula-tion demographics along with personal and course characteristics are factors that contribute to lower persistence of online students, the role of supporting student services may be underestimated.

Students who successfully complete online courses but fail to develop academic self-confidence, motivation to achieve goals, insti-tutional commitment, and social support may still be at risk of drop-ping out (Lotkowski, Robbins, & Noeth, 2004). Research reports that a crucial factor to student persistence is the quality of the student's relationship with at least one person in the university community, often the academic advisor or supervisor (Lotkowski et al., 2004; Park & Choi, 2009).

While studies on retention abound, research on the impact of advising strategies on academic achievement and persistence, particu-larly relating to online learning, are limited. This chapter shares one university's journey to build online academic advising, based on the premise that "student success must be at the core of all institutional work and decision making; therefore, academic advising is critical to the success of higher education" (Drake, 2011, p. 12).

Academic Advising

Academic advisors connect students with appropriate academic learning experiences as well as services such as orientation and reg-istration, financial planning and management, library and bookstore, academic and career counselling, social support services, and techni-cal support (Floyd & Casey-Powell, 2004). The advising relationship provides individualized recommendations to utilize relevant student services that will best support the particular student's success. Aca-demic advising is a continuous process of assisting the student in identifying and clarifying plans, next steps, and goals, and then evalu-ating how academic progress is contributing to achieving their life goals. Advisors advocate for their students, interacting with student services provided through various campus departments to meet online student needs.

A review of literature suggests that the most important advising strategy for online students is to build caring relationships with students wherever they are, flexibly using communication modes that work best (Bettinger, Boatman, & Long, 2013; McGivney, 2004). Online students add studies to already-full lives, juggling professional and personal responsibilities. When life detours, study plans may be aborted and restarted numerous times. Effective online academic advisors build bridges that foster persistence through meaningful connections from orientation through to graduation. They "use these connections to help the students feel connected to something larger than just the computer, their online course, or the school's web site" (Varney, 2009, p. 1).

Excellent academic advising is concerned with more than personal vocational decisions; it is more than prescribing the path through courses to program completion. The developmental perspective positions academic advisors as facilitators of "the student's rational processes, environmental and interpersonal interactions, behavioural awareness and problem-solving, decision-making and evaluation skills" (Crookston, 1994, p. 5). In this view, advisory roles include aspects of mentoring, coaching, encouraging, teaching, supervising, and connecting to the right resources at the right time for a particular student.

Given the mentoring and coaching value of advising, the literature indicates appreciative and proactive advising as strategies that increase student success. Drawing from the fields of constructivism, positive psychology, and appreciative inquiry, appreciative advising makes use of collaborative dialogue and advisor-guided reflection (Bloom, Hutson, He, & Konkle, 2013), using open-ended questions to help the student maximize achievement of their study goals using their strengths (Redfern, 2008; Truschel, 2007).

Six phases of appreciative advising create caring relationships to support students, using any combination of technologies (phone, instant messaging, email, video conference, etc.) to communicate at a distance. Phase one, *Disarm*, builds trusting relationships through friendly interest and small talk. In phase two, *Discover*, the advisor learns about the student's situation and interests. In phase three, *Dream*, the advisor and student work together to clarify strengths and personal calling or professional goals. This will include determining the best program of study to achieve desired goals. During phase four, *Design*, plans are made to achieve the defined goals, realistically considering the student's unique context. Decisions about how many classes to take each term and the sequence of courses can now be made. In phase five, *Deliver*, the advisor supports the student in completing the next step. Inviting the student to email or text when they have completed their first assignment provides an opportunity to offer praise and connection to available student services as/when needed. Phase six, *Don't Settle*, encourages the student to expand their horizons, from completing a course and through a program, to graduate studies or new work opportunities. Through all six phases of appreciative advising or education, which are repeated as needed through the student's study journey, open-ended questions are used to foster a nurturing environment and build reflective, trusting relationships (Bloom et al, 2013; Hensley & Kinser, 2001; Howell, 2010; Redfern, 2008; Shirley, 2012; Truschel, 2007).

As non-traditional students pursue online education, a wealth of prior formal and informal learning along with personal strengths can be harnessed through an approach that appreciates their journey and customizes their path to achieve their goals as much as possible. However, busy adults forget and are not always able to articulate their career path or study goals. Adding proactive advising strategies to an appreciative approach can fill this gap.

Proactive or intrusive advising increases the effectiveness of academic advising as it enhances student preparedness to build academic skills. Taking the initiative to build a relationship in which expectations for advising are set from the start is key. Proactive advisors prepare for appointments that intentionally scaffold the student's progress through asking key questions, then connecting the student with appropriate support services. Follow up and accessibility are core components to this strategy (Cannon, 2013), with advisors being proficient and flexible in using a variety of communication tools (Lorenzetti, 2004; McGivney, 2004; Simpson, 2006, 2008) to reach and coach the student at key points in their online learning journey.

Perhaps the most comprehensive articulation of effective advising, reflecting both appreciative and proactive strategies, is NACADA's (2010) *Distance Education Advising Commission Standards for Advising Distance Learners*. Of the fourteen standards, the following relate to this persistence study:

- "Offer a minimum set of core services which assist distance students in identifying and achieving their education goals
- Employ a myriad of technologies in the delivery of distance education and related services
- Provide an orientation to introduce new students to the distance education environment
- Provide appropriate student support services for distance students as they would for students on campus
- Provide a single point of contact for the services commonly accessed by distance students
- Create opportunities for connection and community with the institution, faculty, staff, and other students
- Respond to the unique needs of distance learning students, rather than expecting them to fit within the established organizational structure" (NACADA, 2010, p. 1)

These standards provide a checklist of activities academic advisors can facilitate or engage in to maximize persistence to timely graduation. Notably, *continuous evaluation and improvement of student services* is one of these advising standards that is also an essential component to growing quality online services.

Persistence Study

Building on this literature review of best strategies and standards for academic advising, the rest of this chapter shares one university's mixed methods action research for the purpose of improving online student services in general and academic advising, as one aspect of student services. The aim of the study was to better understand what made some students continue or persist to complete online programs.

Methodology

This mixed methods action research triangulated quantitative and qualitative data from annual academic advisor evaluations, advisor conversations and email interviews. Data was analysed to answer exploratory questions about the impact of advising strategies, and personal factors identified as contributing to student persistence, and whether these held true in the online learning environment.

To better understand online students' responses to annual advisor surveys, an email interview format was added because it provided the flexibility needed for working adults in multiple time zones, yet built in a personal touch through the mode of communication most often used with their trusted academic advisor; confidentiality and anonymity in reporting was promised. The advisor, as action researcher, could then triangulate the emergent themes from qualitative reflective responses with quantitative data accessed through the student information system, and with qualitative advisor-student communication records documenting the student's goals, context of study, shared personal challenges, and solutions. This disciplined process of reflective inquiry by the advisor as chief researcher follows the methodology of educational action research.

Setting and participants

Undergraduate online degree students within 30 credits of completing or having graduated in the past year were asked to participate in an asynchronous written interview. Questions were emailed as open-ended interview prompts, requesting reflection on their personal experience completing degrees online through a small, diverse, Christian university in the United States.

Aged 23 to 68, with an average of 38 years of age, all but one student worked full-time, adding part-time study. Two of the three recent graduates who responded had started graduate programs; the third had a new position, made possible through degree completion. All were residing in the United States but with a mix of citizenships and educational backgrounds.

The female majority reflected in both US higher education demographics and European distance education students (Schneller & Holmberg, 2014b) was reflected in the participant gender ratio of just over half being female. Notably, this did not reflect the two-thirds male majority of this institution's online student demographics, attributed to the greater male interest/self-selection into the largest undergraduate degree, BA Religion. Possibly, the disproportionate number of females reflected their willingness to write interview responses.

Eleven of the twenty distance degree students invited to participate responded, most with rich responses to each question, connecting to key experiences already shared with their advisor through video, phone, or email communication. Reflection on responses from the first seven respondents, who had graduated or applied to graduate in that term, and on further literature review, prompted extending an invitation to online students within 30 credits of graduating. The second group were given the same interview questions as the first group, adding an additional section asking them to rank seven factors identified in the literature review as contributing to the persistence of online students. Five of the fourteen students invited in the second group responded. While the small number of participants allowed the researcher to consider each individual's context, the qualitative study limits generalizability.

Interview questions

In order to explore the diverse factors possibly influencing persistence, interview questions probed for choice of institution, timing of studies, significance and types of support, challenges, impact on vocation, and advice for new online students. Open-ended questions allowed for in-depth answers as students freely wrote whatever came to mind. Response implied consent to a confidential review of data and anonymity in reporting as assured.

Seven questions were included in interviews of both groups:

Why did you choose this university?

    a. How did the university's mission factor in to your decision, if at all?

    b. How did you hear about the university at first?

Why did you choose to study at this time of your life?

    a. If encouraged by your employer, family, or others, what kind of support did they provide?

    b. How significant was this support to your success?

What challenges have you had to overcome in order to persist to this point?

If you could start this study journey again, what would you plan to do differently?

How have your studies impacted your vocation and why?

What has been the most rewarding part of your studies and why?

What advice would you give a student considering studies online?

The second group was also asked to rank seven factors from 1 (most important to me) to 7 (least important to me or rarely used/ needed) as they related to their journey to program completion online (i.e. persistence to graduation). Responses to this survey were collected via a google form. Student persistence factors were worded and listed as follows:

1. Increased online faculty instruction/faculty-student interaction
2. Meaningful feedback to students
3. Transfer credits received by students
4. Maintaining an adequate GPA/last online course grade
5. Student support – academic & financial advising
6. Student orientation online & tech support
7. Student self-discipline

Findings and Discussion

The data analysis process featured reflecting on emerging themes from both interviews in this study. These findings were sifted through data from annual advising evaluations, literature review, advising reflective practice, and documentation, as evident in the discussion linked to findings organized by interview questions through this section.

Responses indicated that students selected this university's online program for two main reasons. Students working full-time most often explained their choice as "best financial and most convenient"; returning to complete a degree started through the university was a close second. Demographic data and advisor conversations added the reality that several of these students are indeed living in remote locations, making online education their only choice without relocating. Readmitted students all noted alignment of the university's Christian mission with their personal mission as an important part of choosing to return.

Employer financial assistance and/or release time were key support factors facilitating persistence. Family emotional support and childcare assistance were considered essential: "It is very important to know that those closest to you are standing behind your decisions." And while work and family support were essential, they were also the "main obstacles" that "suck your time away from classes and studying." Social, emotional, psychological, and financial support examples were shared in clearly appreciative phrases. In both responses to this interview question and the past year's advisor survey responses, an academic advisor was noted as contributing more than academic support, valued for their dedication to connecting and caring beyond what was expected at a distance.

The reasons for studying at this time reflected three themes. Half the students intentionally chose this institution and program of study for employment reasons. A third had chosen this Christian university's online program in fulfilment of a personal calling or career change. Some were fulfilling personal lifetime education goals. Word of mouth information and online research contributed to their choice to study now and through this university.

All of the above findings are corroborated in literature, succinctly summarized in the IDEAL (Impact of Distance Education on Adult Learning) project report on student characteristics (Schneller & Holmberg, 2014b). Learning to use new technology to study and communicate was mentioned by several students as a challenge in transition to distance education. Given the opportunity to study in a different way, about half noted preference for studying on campus but felt the online format fit their situation best at this time. Appreciative advising helps students value the opportunity to learn new technologies required to study online, building skills transferable to the workplace. Proactive strategies recognize student fear of new and unknown aspects of studying online and provide timely scaffolding.

Students also reflected on the impact of their online studies on their vocation. A younger adult's response is representative: "Being more educated I feel impacts your life in general no matter what the topics. They help provide a fuller understanding of life. Writing papers and learning also helps develop critical thinking which I believe has helped me excel in my workplace." Completing a degree for employment benefit was celebrated or anticipated by those reporting this reason for studying. Appreciative and proactive advising strategies help students in career preparation.

Participants from the second group responded to the same email interview questions and a new section ranking seven student persistence factors. Ranking of these factors varied, related to individual context. However, clusters were evident. The quality of student support through advising and faculty-student interaction were most important to continuing online learning. The importance of student self-discipline, meaningful feedback given to students in online courses, and student orientation online and tech support, formed a second cluster. Those who were completing online degrees due to employment pressure gave higher priority to how transfer credits were articulated; those who did not mention employment as a reason for persisting to degree completion, ranked articulation of transfer credits lowest. Grade point average (GPA) or course grade was of little import to all but one of these online students. For adults who stepped out of higher education, goals of graduate school and professional advancement pressed for completion over grades, making the *dream phase* of appreciative advising a key starting point and motivator in implementing study plans.

While further data collection could increase validity of this action research, student responses gathered were supported by a qualitative study in which a panel of 20 experts in online higher education identified three factors that may affect student persistence in online programs (Heyman, 2010). Similar to the two clusters ranked highest by students in this study, student support and student connection with the institution, quality of interaction between faculty and students, and student self-discipline were significant to online persistence in Heyman's study (2010).

Findings of the larger European IDEAL study of adult students are also of interest. This study found that students perceived that online learning materials and administrative support were important to online success and voted their providers as giving good service in these areas. But factors of moral or psychological support and opportunities to interact with teachers and other students were ranked as less important, and related performance by the providers as weaker in these areas (Schneller & Holmberg, 2014b). While it would appear that expectations for online student service (including academic advising) are affected by contextual or socio-cultural factors not addressed in either study, it is notable that student support and quality of educator-learner interaction were included in both the American and European studies.

Praxis

Literature review and mixed methods action research informed decisions for improvement of supporting technology as well as protocols and training of professional and faculty advisors. Findings also prompt us to continually improve services to the growing and global online student population.

Academic advisors are being prepared to assist online students across all phases of their connection to the university in order to provide the preferred single point of contact and depth of relationship best for online student success. This includes being the first point of contact once admitted, for questions about policy and procedure, degree planning and course selection, connecting with university resources for student success, facilitating positive growth through failures, scaffolding for increasing self-management, career counselling, and steps to graduation.

Student communication, documentation, and follow-up is currently managed through a combination of institutional and personally selected tools, resulting in variations in advising practice. Advisor surveys and distance degree student interviews are providing data to better understand the impact of academic advising where advisors have embraced appreciative and proactive or intrusive advising approaches.

Appreciative advising strategies now in use include building a positive, encouraging relationship; affirming positive study skills; and development of technology skills enabling successful online learning. Academic advisors help online students envision success through honest reflection and action planning following failure or returning after stepping out of higher education for several years. They reassure students by sharing models for success in their situation and celebrate successful completion of each term of study.

Proactive advising strategies implemented include discussing scheduling to maximize success, addressing remediation as soon as needed, referring online students to campus and online support services, acting on early alerts by professors, reviewing mid-term grades, and mandating academic coaching sessions or educational assessment for probationary students. Using a variety of technology tools to track student progress increases presence, providing opportunity to individualize student support to maximize their success.

Compared to all students responding to this university's 2015 advisor evaluation survey, a higher percentage of at-risk and online adult students indicated that they understood their degree requirements, attended advising appointments, and that their advisors connected them with support services as needed. This was found to be one positive indicator that the full-time academic advisors, consistently using appreciative and proactive strategies, are more positively impacting the students they advise than the faculty advisors who are not specifically trained in or using these approaches.

Qualities online students appreciated about their academic advisors were respectful, supportive, knowledgeable, and understanding of goals. Several students resonated with these quotes: "my advisor really cares and thinks outside the box to kindly introduce a better way to do things"; "truly there 24/7 to help and assist". One online student recommended that "the advisor follow the student" instead of being "passed from department to department"; a suggestion supported by NACADA's standards for online academic advising and current practice at this university for faculty already in the role of academic advisor for online undergraduate students.

Conclusion

Results from continuing exploratory and mixed methods action research at one small, internationally-diverse Christian university indicate that appreciative and proactive academic advising approaches implemented with undergraduate online programs increased student persistence to degree completion. Continued action research including data metrics from the learning management system is recommended, along with continual experimentation with the expanding array of instructional and communication technology to support student success through innovative academic advising for students studying online.

Glynis Bradfield

Currently, Glynis Bradfield is the director of distance and non-traditional student services at Andrews University. Her diverse educational experience includes teaching in four countries across two continents at all levels, innovation in educational resource management for Seventh-day Adventist education globally (see circle.adventist.org and educators.adventist.org), and religious curriculum and assessment work through youth ministry and her doctoral research (see growingfruitfuldisciples.com). Invested in mixed methods educational design research, she continues studies in the areas of Christian spiritual development, as well as persistence in precollege and online non-traditional student populations.

References

Bettinger, E. P., Boatman, A., & Long, B. T. (2013). Student supports: Developmental education and other academic programs. *The Future of Children, 23*(1), 93-115. doi:10.1353/foc.2013.0003

Bloom, J. L., Hutson, B. L., He Y., & Konkle, E (2013). Appreciative education. *New Directions for Student Services,* 2013(143), 5-18. doi:10.1002/ss.20055

Cannon, J. (2013). Intrusive advising 101: How to be intrustive without intruding. *Academic Advising Today, 36*(1).

Carnoy, M., Rabling, B., Castano-Munoz, J., Duart Montoliu, J., & Sancho-Vinuesa, T. (2012). Who attends and completes virtual universities: The case of the open University of Catalonia (UOC). *Higher Education, 63*(1), 53-82. doi:10.1007/s10734-011-9424-0

Crookston, B. B. (1994). A developmental view of academic advising as teaching. *NACADA Journal, 14*(2), 5-9.

Drake, J. K. (2011). The role of academic advising in student retention and persistence. *Wiley Online Library* (July-August). doi:10.1002/abc.20062

Floyd, D. L., & Casey-Powell, D. (2004). New roles for student support services in distance learning. *New Directions for Community Colleges* (128).

Harrell, I. L., & Bower, B. L. (2011). Student characteristics that predict persistence in community college online courses. *American Journal of Distance Education, 25*(3), 178-191. doi:10.1080/08923647.2011.590107

Hensley, L. G., & Kinser, K. (2001). Rethinking adult learner persistentence: Implications for counselors. *Adultspan, 3*(2).

Hershkovitz, A., & Nachmias, R. (2011). Online persistence in higher education web-supported courses. *Internet & Higher Education, 14*(2), 98-106. doi:10.1016/j.iheduc.2010.08.001

Heyman, E. (2010). Overcoming student retention issues in higher education online programs. *Online Journal of Distance Learning Administration, XIII*(IV).

Howell, N. G. (2010). *Appreciative advising from the academic advisor's viewpoint: A qualitative study.* Dissertation. University of Nebraska, Lincoln. Retrieved from http://digitalcommons.unl.edu/cgi/viewcontent.cgi?article=1021&context=cehsedaddiss

Kena, G., Aud, S., Johnson, F., Wang, X., Zhang, J., Rathbun, A., & Dziuba, A. (2014). *The condition of education 2014.* International Center for Education Statistics. Retrieved from http://nces.ed.gov/pubs2014/2014083.pdf

Knapp, L. G., Kelly-Reid, J. E., & Ginder, S. A. (2012). Enrollment in post-secondary institutions, Fall 2010; Financial statistics, fiscal year 2010; and graduation rates, selected cohorts, 2002-07. National Center for Education Statistics. Retrieved from http://nces.ed.gov/pubs2012/2012280.pdf

Lokken, F., & Mullins, C. (2014). Trends in eLearning: Tracking the impact of eLearning at community colleges Instructional Technology Council.

Lorenzetti, J. P. (2004). Proactive academic advising for distance students. *Distance Education Report, 8*(20), 4-6.

Lotkowski, V. A., Robbins, S. B., & Noeth, R. J. (2004). The role of academic and non-academic factors in improving college retention. *ACT Policy Report* (pp. 31): ACT, Australia.

McGivney, V. (2004). Understanding persistence in adult learning. *Open Learning, 19*(1).

NACADA. (2010). *Distance education advising commission standards for advising distance learners.* Retrieved from http://www.nacada.ksu.edu/Portals/0/Commissions/C23/Documents/DistanceStandards.pdf

Park, J. H., & Choi, H. J. (2009). Factors influencing adult students' decision to drop out or persist in online learning. *Educational Technology & Society, 12*(4), 207-217.

Redfern, K. (2008). Appreciative advising and the nontraditional student. *The Mentor, 10.*

Ross, T., Kena, G., Rathbun, A., KewalRamani, A., Zhang, J., Kristapovich, P., & Manning, E. (2012). *Higher education: Gaps in access and persistence study.* National Center for Education Statistics. Retrieved from http://nces.ed.gov/pubs2012/2012046.pdf

Schneller, C., & Holmberg, C. (2014a). Distance education in European higher education - the offer. *Report 1 (of 3) of the IDEAL (Impact of distance education on adult learning) project.* Norway: UNESCO Institute for Lifelong Learning, International Council for Open and Distance Education, StudyPortals B.V. Retrieved from https://files.eric.ed.gov/fulltext/ ED560484.pdf

Schneller, C., & Holmberg, C. (2014b). Distance education in European higher education - the students. *Report 2 (of 3) of the IDEAL (Impact of distance education on adult learning) project.* Norway: UNESCO Institute for Lifelong Learning, International Council for Open and Distance Education, StudyPortals B.V. Retrieved from https://files.eric.ed.gov/fulltext/ ED560485.pdf

Shirley, J. V. (2012). *The impact of appreciative advising on community college transfer students*. Dissertation. Western Carolina University. Retrieved from http://libres.uncg.edu/ir/wcu/f/ Shirley2012.pdf

Simpson, O. (2006). Predicting student success in open and distance learning. *Open Learning, 21*(2), 125-138. doi:10.1080/02680510600713110

Simpson, O. (2008). Motivating students in open and distance learning: Do we need a new theory of learner support? *Open Learning, 23*(3), 159-170. doi:10.1080/02680510802419979

Truschel, J. H. (2007). Using appreciative inquiry in advising at-risk students: Moving from challenge to success. *The Mentor, 9*.

Varney, J. (2009). *Strategies for success in distance advising*. Retrieved from http://www.nacada.ksu.edu/Resources/Clearinghouse/View-Articles/Distance-advising-strategies.aspx

4. Integrating the Scholarship of Teaching, Learning, and Assessment into One Institution's Home-grown Professional Learning Resources

Maria Northcote. Director of the Centre for Advancement of the Scholarship of Teaching and Learning. Avondale College of Higher Education, Cooranbong, Australia. Corresponding Author: maria.northcote@avondale.edu.au

Anthony Williams. Director of Academic Governance and Performance, The University of Wollongong Global Enterprises, Wollongong, Australia. Adjunct Professor, Avondale College of Higher Education, Cooranbong, Australia.

Kevin Petrie. Dean of the Faculty of Education, Business and Science. Avondale College of Higher Education, Cooranbong, Australia

John Seddon. Research Project Manager. Avondale College of Higher Education, Cooranbong, Australia

Sherene Hattingh. Primary Education Course Convenor, Faculty of Education, Business and Science. Avondale College of Higher Education, Cooranbong, Australia

Abstract

Many professional learning (PL) programs in universities aspire to support tertiary educators to perform duties associated with teaching, student learning, and assessment. Additionally, because much of a university academic's work is associated with conducting scholarly research and supervising students' research, PL programs also need to provide support associated with supervision and research activities. Faced with these multiple PL demands, one small Australian higher education institution developed a suite of resources to support faculty teaching staff and researchers in their professional capacities using a heuristic (self-determined) approach to resource development. The content of the resources drew on the principles of the Scholarship of Teaching and Learning (SoTL) and a participatory research methodology was adopted to develop the resources. This chapter outlines almost a decade of scholarly work that has resulted in the construction of a collection of PL resources which have been developed to improve the quality of the institution's SoTL and research.

Purpose

The purpose of this chapter is to provide an account of a suite of home-grown professional learning (PL) resources that were created at one small higher education institution in Australia across almost one decade within the organisational structures of a number of funded research projects. These resources were designed to support researcher education, postgraduate supervision, and the scholarship of teaching and learning (SoTL), especially in the areas of online teaching and authentic learning. This collection of PL resources has been developed for the purposes of improving the quality of the institution's SoTL and research. The theoretical framework is also described, including the pedagogical principles on which the resources were built and the research methodology adopted to develop these resources. The chapter does not report on the evaluation of the use and impact of these resources but the outcomes of such evaluations have been reported elsewhere (for example, Boddey & Northcote, 2015; Northcote & Williams, 2014; Northcote, Williams, Carton, Petrie, & Lemke, 2017, in press; Petrie, Anderson, de Waal, et al., 2016).

Theoretical Framework

SoTL, especially the type of scholarship espoused by Trigwell (2013) and Boyer (1990), provided the foundational core on which the PL resources outlined in this chapter were designed. The SoTL commonly refers to the practice of inquiring about teaching and learning, and then sharing and publicizing the findings of such inquiries to enhance the quality of teaching and, consequently, the quality of the students' learning experiences. Specifically, the nature and content of the resources outlined in this chapter are intended to support high quality teaching, learning, research, and assessment, and inquiry into these areas at the institution, in ways that promote sharing of knowledge and public scrutiny of the resources. Trigwell (2013) suggests teaching and learning become more scholarly "when teaching is seen as scholarly and inquiring and when it is made public and peer reviewed" (p. 95), reminding us that the whole purpose of the SoTL is "to enhance students' experience of learning" (p. 95). Trigwell's

(2013) suggestions along with Boyer's (1990) definition of the SoTL as being a systematic inquiry of teaching and learning that is shared and open to public scrutiny and evaluation, all align well with the current focus of Avondale College of Higher Education. The institution is currently harnessing its resources to build a research-intensive institution that augments a strong scholarly culture in which teaching and learning are highly valued by all stakeholders of the institution. For a higher education institution that is on track to becoming a university, the SoTL approach provides a strong theoretical foundation to guide the advancement of scholarly teaching and learning, and goes hand-in-hand with SoTL-informed research practices. The SoTL pedagogical principles underlying the content of the resources were complemented by a participatory research methodology that was adopted to develop the resources. This methodological approach is outlined below.

Research Methodology

The resources outlined in this chapter were devised and created by adopting participatory forms of research and evaluation methodologies. These methodological approaches were characterized by involving as many stakeholders as possible in the design, development, and evaluation of the resources. The primary form of research methodology used to develop these resources was a utilisation-focused evaluation research methodology (Patton, 2012, 2015), an approach that is particularly helpful in engaging stakeholders and resource-users in the process of developing educational resources. Through mixed methods research approaches, data were gathered by conducting focus groups, questionnaires, and interviews with undergraduate and postgraduate students, faculty members, postgraduate supervisors, and administrative staff. For some resources, panels of experts were also consulted to gather specialist advice about the nature, content, and presentation of the resources. Data collected from these various sources were compared, analysed, and triangulated to ensure the credibility and trustworthiness of the findings identified during the development of each resource (Guba & Lincoln, 1989). Further comparative analysis with relevant literature was conducted to ensure the resources were aligned with current best practice in the field of PL and higher education.

The use of Patton's (2012, 2015) utilisation-focused evaluation research approach ensured that processes adopted to design, develop, and evaluate the resources were evidence-based, being informed by locally gathered research data. In each case, these processes were actively researched and data were gathered in an ongoing way to inform the continual appraisal of these resources. This ensured that the resources themselves were characterized by the SoTL (Boyer, 1990; Kreber & Kanuka, 2013; Trigwell, Martin, Benjamin, & Prosser, 2000). Because many of the resources were intended to reach faculty members across disciplines and to present knowledge that was applicable in nature, they represent examples of the scholarship of integration, the scholarship of teaching, and the scholarship of application, as described by Boyer (1990). Each of the resources outlined in this chapter undergo regular evaluation. Although this is not the focus of this chapter, the outcomes of the resource evaluations have been reported elsewhere.

Results: Homegrown Professional Learning Resources

Over the past eight years, scholars, researchers, administrators, and educators at Avondale have worked together to design and develop a range of scholarly PL resources. The funding and support for these projects has been provided mainly through external funding from competitive grants provided by the Office for Learning and Teaching in Australia. These external grants were supplemented by in-house funding and in-kind support. Each resource is now described.

The Researcher's Little Helper

The development of the *Researcher's Little Helper* has provided a central online repository that both students and staff can access to support their research endeavours (see Figure 4.1). Housed within Moodle, the Learning Management System (LMS) used by the institution, the structure of this resource is organized into topics that cover the key skills that are central to successful academic research, including: selecting a research topic, writing a literature review, methodological approaches, and ethical considerations. These topics are specific to the needs of higher degree research (HDR) students as they plan and complete their thesis/dissertation, including: advice about developing a research proposal, tips for writing a thesis/ dissertation, examples of completed theses/dissertations, and links relevant to the institution's policies. In addition to providing support for the development of core research skills, the site provides links to resources that assist in embedding a researcher into a sustainable and active research community, such as sites that promote collaboration with other researchers, as well as sites that provide advice about reporting research and securing research funding. For those faculty members who wish to develop further skills in the supervision of higher degree research students, a link within the site provides access to the newly developed *Research Training Support Framework*, outlined in the following section of this chapter.

Figure 4.1 The Researcher's Little Helper homepage.
A website within Avondale's Moodle

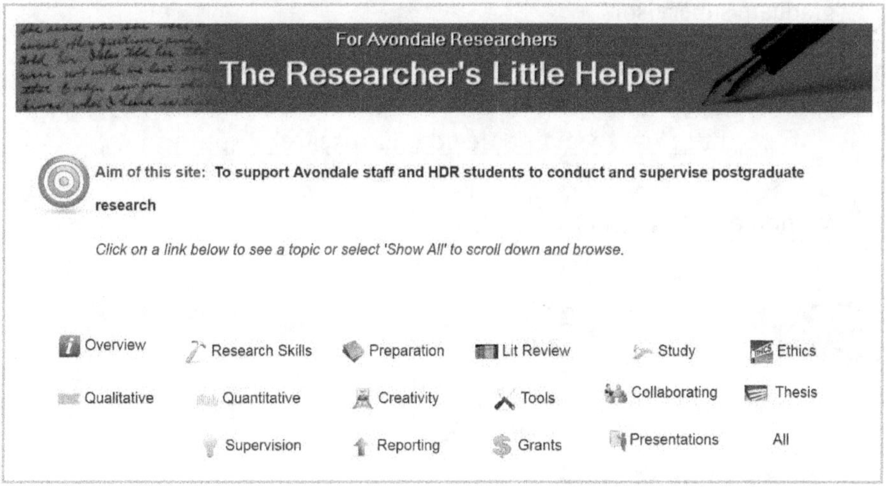

Research Training Support Framework

The *Research Training Support Framework* was developed to encourage and empower current and potential supervisors of higher degree research students (Petrie, Anderson, Carton, et al., 2016) (see Figure 4.2). The development of the Framework was funded by an Extension Grant from the Office for Learning and Teaching in Australia. The Framework was developed in collaboration with a number of national and international experts (Petrie et al., 2015). Initiated in response to identified needs of both staff and students, it is based on the premise that developing a pedagogy of supervision (Nulty, Kiley, & Meyer, 2009) is central to supporting an active institutional research culture. The Framework provides advice for each step of a typical HDR student's progression through their degree, beginning with admission into an HDR program, the selection of a supervisor, and the subsequent confirmation process that is required in many HDR programs in Australian universities. The Framework focuses on skills specific to guiding a student in managing their research project, the development of appropriate writing skills, and the process of publishing and presenting research findings. A number of brief fact-sheets are included in each of the Framework's stages, providing advice within areas such as the supervision of part-time students, working effectively with distance students, and cross-cultural considerations. Each area of the Framework provides links to other Avondale web-pages (e.g., policies) that guide students' progression through their postgraduate degree and set institutional expectations for their post-graduate supervisors.

Figure 4.2 A screenshot of the research training support framework website. It is available at
http://www.avondale.edu.au/research-training

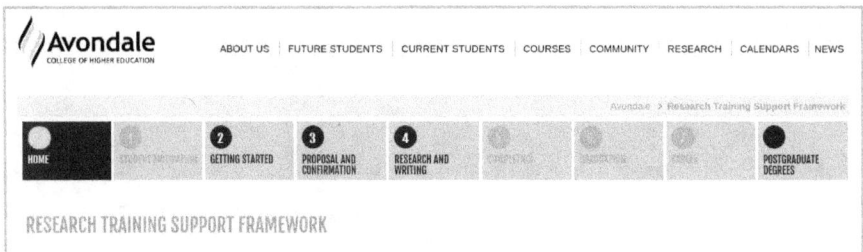

Moodle's Little Helper

Moodle's Little Helper was initiated in 2012 and developed to assist academic staff with their online teaching and course design (see Figure 4.3). Moodle is the LMS platform used at this institution and so the plain and coherent name of this tool was chosen to easily identify it when needed by staff. This self-help PL resource provides accessible and flexible instructions and resources in an online context to assist faculty members in 12 identified areas related to online teaching and online course design (Northcote & Boddey, 2014), namely: setting up courses, structuring a course, uploading materials, promoting learner interactivity, assessment portals, media enhancements, examples of best practice, quality of online courses, contacting and monitoring students, Turnitin, literature about online learning, and PL workshops. The resource is designed in a way that enables faculty members to instantly access the area in which they require help. Quick access is enabled through a hyperlinked menu to video tutorials, text-based instructional resources, best practice showcases, course exemplars, and workshop materials (Northcote & Boddey, 2014). Staff access this online resource tool regularly and independently for guidance and help as required. This resource is regularly monitored and updated for ongoing faculty PL, and for teaching and course design developments.

**Figure 4.3 The Moodle's Little Helper homepage.
A website within Avondale's Moodle.**

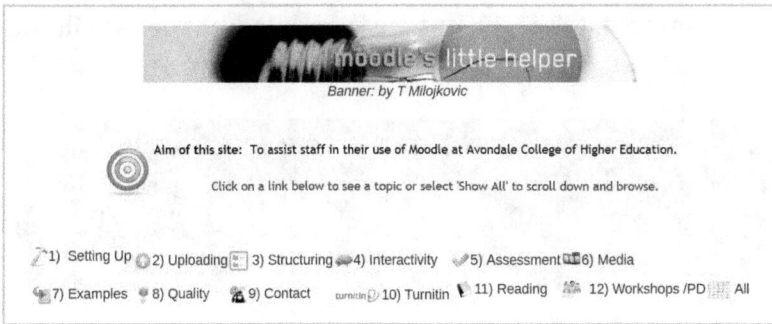

Assessment @ Avondale

Many universities, both in Australia and internationally, have put much effort into providing cutting-edge resources for assessment (Cox, Bradford, & Miller, 2016; Dawson, 2015; The Higher Education Academy, 2012). In response to this trend Avondale created an assessment website (see Figure 4.4). The *Assessment@Avondale* (A@A) website has been funded by internal in-kind support from the Office of Academic and Research of Avondale. The website aims to offer a collection of high quality resources for faculty members to use in their consideration of best practice in the design and use of assessment tasks in their courses. A@A is a portal that provides a collection of assessment resources which are mainly pre-existing resources from other universities and higher education sources. The audience is intended to be those involved in teaching and assessing higher education students at Avondale. As the resource develops in the future it will expand its audience by offering information to help students make the most of their assessment tasks, grades, and the various forms of feedback lecturers offer them.

The A@A website elucidates the important areas of good assessment alongside references to the relevant institutional policies affecting assessment at Avondale. It is comprised of sections covering principles and standards (Boud & Associates, 2010; Shapland, 2011); assessment construction and processes (Biggs, 2014; Kandlbinder, 2014); a large collection of examples and types of assessment, student understanding and reflection tips, and PL and research resources. The website supports those involved in learning, teaching, and assessment, with easy access to information across the multi-faceted nature of the modern approach to assessment taken at Avondale.

Figure 4.4 Assessment @ Avondale website. Available at: http://assessment.avondale.edu.au

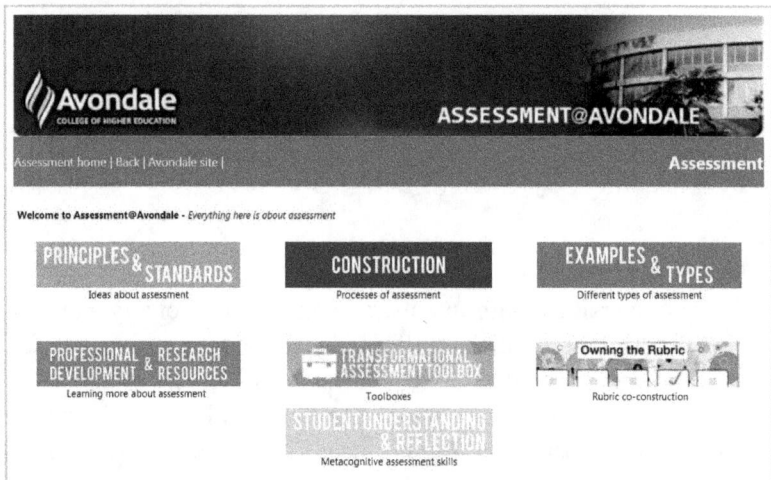

Transformational Assessment Toolbox

The *Transformational Assessment Toolbox* is a collection of Avondale resources and outcomes funded by a Seed Grant from the Office for Learning and Teaching in Australia, and accessed via a tab on the Assessment@Avondale website, presented in the section above (see Figure 4.5). The resource aims to encourage and provide assistance for course designers and lecturers to rethink and plan their assessment feedback process within the higher education sector. This toolbox has four sections. The first section provides the background information on this resource. The second section provides videos and reports of three case studies that used adaptively released assessment feedback (ARAF) strategies in the tertiary education sector. The third section provides direction for the practice and implementation of ARAF strategies through the use of questions, and implementation of staged practical guidelines for pre-semester and during semester practice as well as recommendations on the timing of these. This section also includes suggestions for future research directions in assessment. The fourth and final section of this resource provides detailed information on the research project that initiated this toolbox as well as publications, key readings and other relevant references for ARAF.

Figure 4.5 A screenshot of the transformational assessment toolbox website. It can be accessed at: http://assessment.avondale.edu.au/toolboxtat

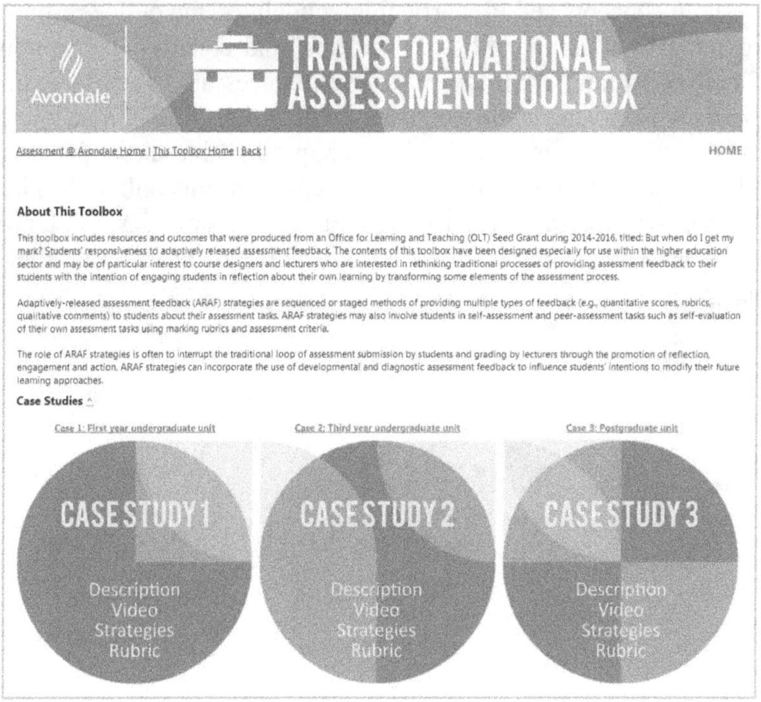

Threshold Concepts for Novice Online Teachers

The *Threshold Concepts for Novice Online Teachers* resource was developed as one of the key products of a research project, funded by a Seed Grant from the Office for Learning and Teaching in Australia, which aimed to identify the threshold concepts that novice online teachers require to teach effectively in online courses (see Figure 4.6). The resource consists of a collection of threshold concepts about online teaching with an explanation of the features of these threshold concepts. For example, two of the threshold concepts noted on the website include "Online course design is critical to the success of online teaching and learning" and "Students can learn without the teacher being present." These threshold concepts represent some key focus points of learning for novice online teachers. Also, practical curriculum design guidelines are provided; these guidelines are intended for use when developing curricula for transformative PL of novice online educators in higher education contexts. In addition to the list of threshold concepts and PL curriculum guidelines, the online resource provides: 1) a summary of the students' and teachers' perceptions of online learning environments; 2) references and links to online resources about threshold concepts; and 3) details of the scholarly publications and presentations that were produced to disseminate the project's findings. Overall, the main intention of this online resource was to provide research-informed guidance for how to design PL programs, activities, and resources for novice online teachers in higher education contexts.

Figure 4.6 A screenshot of the website for Threshold Concepts for Novice Online Teachers. It is available at: http://tcs4nots.avondale.edu.au

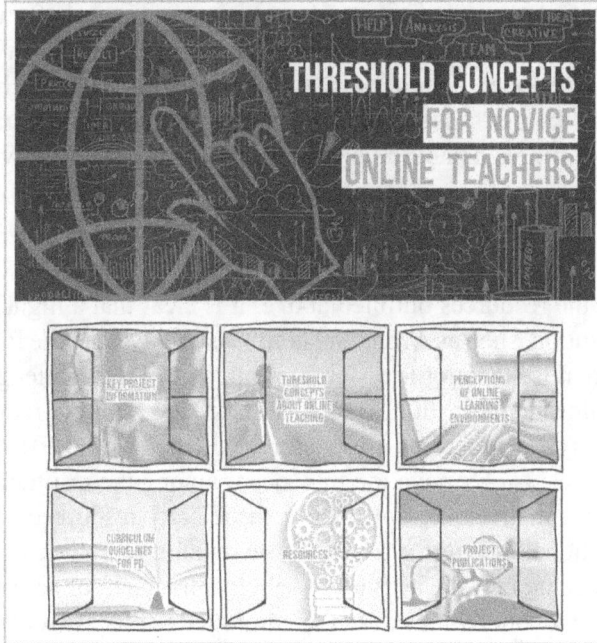

Tutor's Den – Supporting Academic Assistance to Students

The Tutor's Den database has been developed to help those who run a student assistance and academic support centre with a purpose-driven, digitized, and online application. As Avondale already employs the Moodle LMS, its internal database was considered the most appropriate platform to keep the data used to provide tutoring services to students secure. The database supports the documentation of a cycle of assistance provided to students by the tutors at Avondale. The cycle begins with students interacting with lecturers and teachers. When either the students or the lecturer identifies there may be some benefit to be gained through utilizing Avondale's tutoring service, the student can be referred to the service. Tutors work with a student to scaffold the development of their core academic and scholastic skills, increasing their confidence in their capacity to be successful in their degrees.

The various information and reports being generated between students, their teachers, and the tutors can be kept securely in an accessible online place. Secondly, this solution allows the tutoring team to work in collaborative and streamlined ways to support their student clients. Any tutor assisting a student can access records for the individual student case. With up-to-date records, the tutors can respond with interventional learning activities that are most constructive to the individual learner's needs in their current academic circumstances. Utilizing a simple database saves much time and has a positive organising effect on many of the tutor's tasks.

Scholarly Significance

From the resources outlined above, it is clear that a higher education institution, such as Avondale, is advised to invest in the PL of staff in order to raise the profile of scholarship. One of the challenges however within smaller institutions is that often the resources required for high-quality PL programs are lacking (Allen & Kelly, 2015). While isolated pockets of innovation may occur among the institution's faculty, such initiatives are not always sufficiently resourced as part of an institutional strategic plan. Often there is little funding devoted to the enhancement of the activity of scholarship itself, or activities that constitute the foundations of scholarship such as those associated with teacher development, course enhancement, or teaching innovation.

An important part of SoTL is sharing teaching and learning experiences as well as sharing the developed initiative (in this case, a suite of PL resources). Traditionally this was only done in conferences. Institutions need to further develop forums for such activities and build them into their calendar to ensure they become regular components of the institution's calendar of events. The scholars themselves are responsible for sharing such work with peers and colleagues, both within and outside their institution. It is important for a small institution to develop its faculty members' capacity to engage in the activity of communicating their scholarly activities as well as imparting training (Petrie et al., 2015).

The activity of sharing as a scholarly activity is also valuable to other small institutions. As an Adventist institution, Avondale has many sister institutions, especially those in developing countries. There is the potential, especially through such mediums as communicating through video conferencing and accessing online scholarly resources, to involve and engage staff at these institutions in our scholarly sharing times. The Christian education community, which is extensive in Australia, also provides additional sharing opportunities. These communities can be invited to share and contribute to our institutional scholarly activities as well as sharing and using the resources developed as part of that scholarship.

Conclusion

When developing its PL resources, Avondale has been mindful not to fall into the one-size-fits-all trap. Instead, it has been strategic in developing its resources and PL around the themes of diversity. The temptation to make all resources and training narrow for ease has been avoided and the focus of the scholarly and development activities has been directed towards capacity building; enabling staff to take ownership of their own PL and scholarly activities. Avondale offers a diverse range of courses for its size and there are specific disciplinary cultures which exist within the institution. Importantly, not all staff are at the same point in their PL. By developing these resources there have been a number of benefits for Avondale as an institution, including: ongoing individual self-directed support for existing and new staff; a supportive teaching and learning climate; and a positive change in the culture of innovation and scholarship. Intrinsic to the initiatives presented in this chapter is the attribute of ensuring the PL resources are as flexible as possible so as not to exclude staff based on where they are at in their PL journeys. Our desire has always been to enable, empower, and support, rather than to develop uniformity. To sustain this attitude and to sustain the diversity of activities in an institution looking to enhance both its teaching and learning practice, but also its research capacity, scholarly resources must be tailored in ways to support these initiatives.

Acknowledgements

The research projects reported in this chapter were supported by the Office for Learning and Teaching (OLT) in Australia under the Seed Grant Program, grant no. SD15-5203, grant title: Using online teaching threshold concepts in transformative professional learning curricula for novice online educators. In-kind research support was provided by the following institutions: Avondale College of Higher Education, NSW, Australia; Texas A&M University, Texas, USA; and Australian Catholic University, ACT, Australia.

Maria Northcote

Maria Northcote is the Director of the Centre for Advancement of the Scholarship of Teaching and Learning (CASTL) at Avondale College of Higher Education. Maria is an experienced higher education teacher, leader, and researcher and has successfully led an Office for Learning and Teaching Extension Grant through to completion during 2014-2015, and is currently a co-researcher on an Office for Learning and Teaching Seed Grant focusing on higher education assessment. She has led and contributed to a range of research projects in three higher education institutions between 1999 and 2015. Before beginning her work at Avondale, she worked at Newcastle and Edith Cowan Universities, in lecturing, research, and staff development roles. She was recently appointed a Fellow of the Higher Education Research and Development Society of Australasia (HERDSA) in recognition of her service to higher education and her commitment to ongoing professional development to enhance teaching and learning.

Anthony Williams

Anthony Williams recently joined the University of Wollongong Global Enterprises Unit. The unit manages universities and colleges in four locations in Wollongong, Dubai, Hong Kong and Malaysia. Anthony manages the Academic Governance and Performance Portfolio across the institutions. Before taking up the Wollongong assignment, he was at Avondale where he was Vice President (Academic and Research) of Avondale College of Higher Education. He provided leadership in research and scholarship. Prior to that role, he held the position of the Head of School of Architecture and Built Environment at the University of Newcastle NSW. He has extensive experience in project management in the domain of professional education. He is a winner of multiple University Teaching Awards as well as a National Award for Teaching Excellence. He is highly regarded in this area having worked as a curriculum consultant nationally and internationally.

Kevin Petrie

Kevin Petrie is the Dean of the Faculty of Education, Business and Science at Avondale College of Higher Education, NSW, Australia. His research areas include school bullying, classroom management, mathematics education, preservice teacher education, and the professional development of researchers. Before working in higher education, Kevin's experience involved working as a classroom teacher and principal in a number of primary schools. His Doctoral thesis reported on the relationship between student-peer bullying, school climate, and peer popularity.

John Seddon

John Seddon is currently employed as a project manager for a large Office for Learning and Teaching research grant. He has a PhD in tertiary teaching with a keen interest in how we understand student learning and how improving students' understandings of their own learning and assessment can deepen learning experiences and outcomes. John has worked as a university lecturer and a researcher in online education. During his doctoral studies he investigated the role of reflection in the development of new tertiary teachers' conceptions of teaching. Using an online tool he developed as part of his study, the Reflective Practice Website, Jack's study tracked the way in which new tertiary teachers engaged in reflective practices and the effects this had on their conceptions of teaching. Jack has recently facilitated online and face-to-face professional development sessions for higher education teachers who are developing online course design and teaching skills.

Sherene Hattingh

Sherene Hattingh is the Primary Course Convenor in the Faculty of Business, Education, and Science at Avondale College of Higher Education. She has worked in the Primary, Secondary, and Tertiary education sectors as a teacher, lecturer, and administrator. Her education experience spans four countries where she has actively engaged in mainstream classroom teaching, ESL pedagogy, and more recently research in these areas. Her research passions include innovative teaching and learning, internationalisation, ESL students, and pedagogy. She is currently involved in teaching higher education courses on-campus and online where she is creatively working to improve these learning modes and the assessments attached to them.

References

Allen, L., & Kelly, B. B. (2015). Higher education and ongoing professional learning: *Transforming the workforce for children birth through age 8: A unifying foundation.* Washington: National Academies Press.

Biggs, J. (2014). Constructive alignment in university teaching. *HERDSA Review of Higher Education, 1*(1), 5-22.

Boddey, C., & Northcote, M. (2015). Invited presentation: Moodle's Little Helper: Making use of the self-determined principles of heutagogy to support academic staff who are learning to teach online. Paper presented at the MoodleMoot Australia 2015, Monash University, Melbourne, Australia.

Boud, D., & Associates. (2010). Assessment 2020: Seven propositions for assessment reform in higher education. *Sydney.* Australian Learning and Teaching Council (ALTC).

Boyer, E. (1990). *Scholarship reconsidered: Priorities of the professoriate.* New Jersey: The Carnegie Foundation for the Advancement of Teaching.

Cox, K., Bradford, I. W., & Miller, A. (2016). Student assessment in higher education: A handbook for assessing performance. London, UK: Routledge.

Dawson, P. (2015). Assessment rubrics: Towards clearer and more replicable design, research, and practice. *Assessment & Evaluation in Higher Education,* 1-14. doi: 10.1080/02602938.2015.1111294

Guba, E. G., & Lincoln, Y. S. (1989). *Fourth generation evaluation.* Newbury Park, CA: Sage.

Kandlbinder, P. (2014). Constructive alignment in university teaching. *HERDSA News, 36*(3), 5.

Kreber, C., & Kanuka, H. (2013). The scholarship of teaching and learning and the online classroom. *Canadian Journal of University Continuing Education, 32*(2), 109-131.

Northcote, M., & Boddey, C. (2014). Using the self-determined learning principles of heutagogy to support academic staff who are learning to teach online. In B. Hegarty, J. McDonald, & S. K. Loke (Eds.), *Rhetoric and Reality: Critical perspectives on educational technology. Proceedings ASCILITE Dunedin 2014* (pp. 735-739). Dunedin, New Zealand: Australasian Society for Computers in Learning in Tertiary Education (ASCILITE).

Northcote, M., Seddon, J., & Brown, P. (2011). Benchmark yourself: Self-reflecting about online teaching. In G. Williams, P. Statham, N. Brown, & B. Cleland (Eds.), *Changing demands, changing direc-*

tions. Proceedings ASCILITE Hobart 2011 (pp. 904-908). Hobart, Australia: ASCILITE (Australasian Society for Computers in Learning in Tertiary Education).

Northcote, M., & Williams, A. (2014). The Researcher's Little Helper: The design of an enabling online resource for postgraduate students and their supervisors. In M. Picard & A. McCulloch (Eds.), *Proceedings of the 11th Biennial Quality in Postgraduate Research Conference 9-14 April 2014* (pp. 53-67). Adelaide, Australia: University of Adelaide, University of South Australia, and Flinders University.

Northcote, M., Williams, A., Carton, J., Petrie, K., & Lemke, G. (2017, in press). Fit for purpose? The evaluation of a small higher education institution research training support and development framework. *Proceedings of the Ireland International Conference on Education (IICE) Conference.* Dublin, Ireland: Ireland International Conference on Education (IICE).

Nulty, D., Kiley, M., & Meyer, N. (2009). Promoting and recognising excellence in the supervision of research students: An evidence-based framework. *Assessment & Evaluation in Higher Education, 34*(6), 693-707.

Patton, M. Q. (2012). A utilization-focused approach to contribution analysis. *Evaluation, 18*(3), 364-377. doi: 10.1177/1356389012449523

Patton, M. Q. (2015). *Qualitative research and evaluation methods* (4th ed.). Thousand Oaks, CA: Sage.

Petrie, K., Anderson, M., Carton, J., de Waal, K., Lemke, G., Mitchell, B. G., ... Williams, A. (2016). *Designing an innovative system to evaluate a postgraduate supervision support and development framework.* Paper presented at the 12th Biennial Quality in Postgraduate Research Conference: Society, Economy & Communities: 21st Century innovation in Doctoral Education, The National Wine Centre, Adelaide, Australia.

Petrie, K., Anderson, M., de Waal, K., Mitchell, B. G., Northcote, M., Williams, A., & Carton, J. (2016). Designing an innovative system to evaluate a postgraduate supervision support and development framework. In M. Picard & A. McCulloch (Eds.), *Proceedings of the 12th Biennial Quality in Postgraduate Research Conference: Society, Economy & Communities: 21st Century innovation in Doctoral Education* (pp. 132-138). Adelaide, Australia: University of Adelaide, University of South Australia and Flinders University.

Petrie, K., Lemke, G., Williams, A., Mitchell, B. G., Northcote, M., Anderson, M., & de Waal, K. (2015). Professional development of research supervisors: A capacity-building, participatory approach. In

M. Baguley (Ed.), *Australian Association for Research in Education (AARE) Conference 2015* (pp. 1-11). University of Notre Dame Australia, Fremantle, Australia: Australian Association for Research in Education (AARE).

Shapland, N. (2011). Assessment matters! Retrieved from http://app.griffith. edu.au/assessment-matters/

The Higher Education Academy. (2012). A marked improvement: Transforming assessment in higher education. In S. Orr (Ed.). York, UK: The Higher Education Academy.

Trigwell, K. (2013). Evidence of the impact of scholarship of teaching and learning purposes. *Teaching and Learning Inquiry: The ISSOTL Journal, 1*(1), 95-105.

Trigwell, K., Martin, E., Benjamin, J., & Prosser, M. (2000). Scholarship of teaching: A model. *Higher Education Research & Development, 19*(2), 155-168.

5. How are They Going?: A Project to Monitor Student Engagement

Anthony Williams. Director of Academic Governance and Performance, The University of Wollongong Global Enterprises, Wollongong, Australia. Adjunct Professor, Avondale College of Higher Education, Cooranbong, Australia.

Maria Northcote. Director of the Centre for Advancement of the Scholarship of Teaching and Learning. Avondale College of Higher Education, Cooranbong, Australia

John Reddin. Director of Operations mobileLearning.io, North Ryde, Australia

Abstract

The transition from school or work to university studies is not always a smooth change for many students. The university context may appear threatening, strange, and isolating for some students, whether the courses be offered in on-campus or online contexts. While most modern day universities offer a raft of support services for students, including both academic and non-academic services, problems of low retention and high attrition rates still plague some institutions and some sections of particular institutions in the higher education sector. This chapter presents an innovative program that uses technology-supported strategies within a regular learning management system (LMS) to arrest problems that may lead to students withdrawing from their courses. By focusing on students engaged in their first year of study, early intervention systems, known as the Virtual Mentoring Program (VMP) and the Learning Engagement Analytics Platform (LEAP), are presented as examples of how higher education institutions can reduce attrition and increase retention.

Purpose

This chapter considers the rationale for and the processes involved in developing two programs, the Virtual Mentoring Program (VMP) and the Learning Engagement Analytics Platform (LEAP), which aim to enable faculty teaching staff to determine how well their students are engaging with their studies through the application of technology-supported strategies. Through the use of virtual tools, teaching staff are able to see measures of their students' engagement and then provide strategic support to students. By providing guidance and encouragement to students before they reach the point of no return, the programs focused on reducing the risks associated with students withdrawing from their university courses. The programs utilize the institution's learning management system (LMS), extending its potential beyond a transmission of learning materials and learning environments. The LMS is used as a tool to identify students who are experiencing problems or who are not engaging in their studies. Because the actions of such students increase their risk of poor performance or failure, it is this point of risk that the programs aim to address. The strategies are most relevant to online learning students who, by their remoteness, have the potential to add an extra dimension of ambiguity.

Perspective: The Australian Context

Since the 1970s there has been considerable research on issues related to student retention and attrition, and their effect on higher education institutions, as well as on individual students (for example, Masika & Jones, 2016; Tinto, 1999). The motivation for these investigations is not purely pedagogic; it is also pragmatic because universities lose funding if they lose students. Furthermore, attrition rates contribute to a university's reputation. Research confirms the adverse impacts of students withdrawing from university before they obtain their degree and this is evident both nationally (Krause, Hartley, James, & McInnis, 2005; McInnis, Hartley, Polesel, & Teese, 2000) and internationally (Tinto, 1999; Yorke, 2000). In many cases, whether a student's decision to leave university is caused by financial or personal considerations, rising attrition rates may be reduced if intervention occurs early enough. Because of the current higher education contribution scheme (HECS) in Australia, students who withdraw from their university courses often leave with an accrued debt. This provides yet another reason to channel resources into programs that aim to reduce attrition rates.

Pitkethly and Prosser (2001) echo the concerns of McInnis, James, and Hartley (2000) who found that one third of all university students contemplate withdrawing during their first year of study. The work of McInnis, James, et al. (2000) is regarded as seminal and is still relevant as first year students, according to Krause (2005), vacillate between the three sometimes competing tensions of:

- relevancy to themselves of the program they are enrolled in;
- perceptions of themselves as clients (from the marketing and service dimensions of their institution); and
- the disciplinary and academic integrity standards required by academic teaching staff.

These tensions arguably contribute to students withdrawing from university. Several models have been suggested in the effort to explain how student retention and attrition occurs, numerous approaches aimed at reducing attrition have been explored and implemented, and these approaches continue to be investigated, especially for students in the first year of their university studies (Kift, 2015; Krause, 2005; Krause, Hartley, James, & McInnis, 2005; McInnis, Hartley, et al., 2000). Strategies that have been trialled include increasing levels of student engagement, creating learning communities, and implementing strategies to promote academic and social integration. These initiatives have been shown to have a positive impact on student retention (Tinto & Goodsell-Love, 1993; Zhao & Kuh, 2004).

The *Review of Australian Higher Education*, the report commissioned by the Australian Government known as *The Bradley Review* (Bradley, Noonan, Nugent, & Scales, 2008), recommended new directions in higher education including the aim that, by 2020, forty percent of those aged between 25 and 34 years would attain a higher education qualification. For this target to be met, universities need to include students from non-traditional backgrounds in their student populations, contributing to a larger and more diverse student population.

Another factor that complicates the increase in students entering university is the additional factor of online and blended education. Interestingly, students who choose to enrol in online courses are often those who have no experience in tertiary study. They enrol in an online mode of study because it suits their complex lifestyle; they may already be employed and have family commitments. Such students confront the dual issues of learning at the university level and learning in a new learning environment because many of them choose to study online. For universities offering undergraduate degrees, these students with diverse needs, across large classes, present additional challenges.

Within the context described above, many students "hit the wall" and experience difficulty during the early stages of their university studies. For most students, this sense of experiencing difficulty early in their degree soon passes but for some it remains and characterizes the remainder of their studies. For some of these students, difficulties resurface when they face a challenging issue in their lives such as a sickness, mental illness, or a family tragedy. Other students may experience difficulty when they begin studying a subject that they find very challenging or new. Yet again, some students just struggle with their university experience in general; these students become categorized as "students at risk" or students who, because of any number of factors, are not coping. Such students are likely to fail or drop out, or go unnoticed by the staff of the university. These at-risk students require support, whether on a short-term or long-term basis. If not identified by teachers, these problems may lead to a downward spiral of performance and may eventually result in the student disengaging from their studies. In the worst-case scenario, the student may just "fall between the cracks" and withdraw from their studies altogether. Adventist schools and universities pride themselves on the quality of support they provide their students and aim to create an environment that assists students to succeed in their studies by promoting a teaching and learning environment that is exemplified by its holistic learning and pastoral care. Such an environment can also be promoted in an online context.

Research methodology: Using learning analytics to develop a Virtual Mentoring Program

Tinto (1987) established a list of factors that support students and, subsequently, increase retention. Following are some of those factors identified:

- any institutional actions need to be systematic not pockets of initiative with no alignment with institutional programs, systems, and structures;
- programs address students' needs early;
- programs are student-centred; and
- education is the goal of any support programs (p. 139-140).

The important factor, for the purposes of this chapter, is the impact that early intervention has on the potential success of a student and, therefore, retention of that student. In the modern university context, classes are often very large and it is difficult for a lecturer to determine the engagement levels of his or her students, especially early in the semester. The ability to detect students who are not engaging in their coursework is a critical factor in both supporting students who are having difficulties but also in enabling students to be successful in their university studies. Learning analytics, data that indicates student activity and non-activity within an online course system, can be accessed to detect students who may be experiencing difficulties in their studies.

According to Booth (2012), "learning analytics is the measurement, collection, analysis, and reporting of data about learners and their contexts, for purposes of understanding and optimising learning and the environments in which it occurs" (p. 1). The application of learning analytics can potentially be transformative in both tracking and supporting students who experience difficulties in navigating university systems and/or courses. Learning analytics can provide a way for college and university leaders to improve teaching, learning, organizational efficiency, and decision making, and, as a consequence, serve as a foundation for systemic change. By tracking levels of student engagement, the use and analysis of learning analytics provides a level of clarity which can dispel uncertainty around how to allocate resources, develop competitive advantages, and, most importantly, how to improve the quality and value of the student learning experience. The project described here is looking to utilize learning analytics and further develop this data into academic analytics, which is the application of business intelligence in education. The use of academic analytics emphasizes analytics data at institutional, regional, and international levels. Konstantinidis and Grafton (2013) stated: "Analytics marries large data sets, statistical techniques, and predictive modelling. It could be thought of as the practice of mining institutional data to produce 'actionable intelligence" (p. 33). Analytics from LMSs offers a rich source of data for monitoring and predicting the success of learners.

Morris, Finnegan, and Wu (2005) compared basic activities related to LMS participation (e.g., content pages viewed, number of posts) and duration of participation (e.g., hours spent viewing discussion pages and content) in LMSs. They found significant differences between "withdrawers" and "successful completers," concluding that "time spent on task and frequency of participation are important for successful online learning" (p. 221). Macfadyen and Dawson (2010) advocate for early-warning reporting tools that "can flag at-risk students and allow instructors to develop early intervention strategies" (p. 589). This data can serve the purposes of:

- Gaining real-time insight into the engagement and performance of learners; this is important for identifying those students who are at-risk.
- Informing students of their progress against expectations and their peers which benefits their motivation and self-awareness.
- Assisting decision makers in making informed decisions regarding distribution of resources, enabling them to identify those areas of need more readily.

The Project

Following is a brief description of the project in which we are currently immersed. In order to carry out comprehensive analytics, data is generally extracted from various institutional systems, including:

1. **LMS-based engagement reporting tools.** These tools sit within the LMS and generally assist in analysing LMS data only. They provide simple indications of a student's progress. Examples of these tools include Blackboard's Retention Centre and Moodle's Engagement Analytics plug-in.

2. **LMS-centric analytics systems.** These systems were developed by LMS vendors. They combine data from the LMS with data from the Student Information System (SIS) to enable more extensive analysis. Examples of these systems include Blackboard's Analytics for Learn ™ (A4L) and Desire-2Learn's Insights.

3. **SIS-centric analytics systems**. These systems sit alongside the SIS but may also draw in data from the LMS, providing learning analytics alongside wider business intelligence. Examples include Ellucian's Student Retention Performance, and Compass' Promonitor.

4. **Generic business intelligence systems.** These systems were developed to provide better analysis in any business but have not been specifically designed for education. They sit outside both the LMS and SIS but draw data from those and other systems, often in conjunction with a data warehouse. Examples include QlikView, Tableau, IBM Cognos, HP Autonomy, and AWS Quicksight.

The College's partner is the Association for Continuing Higher Education (ACHE) mobileLearning.io who have researched and developed a range of LMS-based engagement reporting tools, LMS-centric analytics systems, and generic business intelligence systems to automate and scale learning analytic processes. To bring these systems into a small institution provides a number of challenges; to assure the successful development and adoption of the systems a project plan needed to be employed. The process established for this project involves a four-stage process including the design, development deployment, and evaluation of the fully integrated Learning Engagement Analytics Platform (LEAP).

The LEAP system will involve behind-the-scene gathering of data which will enable the presentation of data in a readily accessible and usable form for teachers to analyze. This will enable academics to utilize the data in supporting their students. The process of developing the feedback loop for teachers is presented in Figure 5.1:

Figure 5.1 The LEAP system process

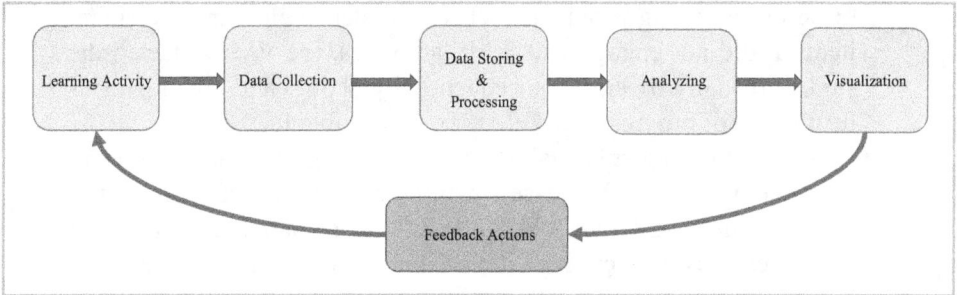

The design of an automated process follows a standard project management process and involves the data from the LMS being interrogated, using predetermined protocols to provide ready access to academics through a dashboard, a data visualization tool displaying the current status of student engagement metrics on a single screen providing easy access for the academics. This process is presented in Figure 5.2:

Figure 5.2 Automated process design

```
┌─────────────┐        ┌─────────────┐        ┌─────────────────────┐
│             │        │             │        │     Dashboard       │
│   Moodle    │ ◄────► │   Custom    │ ◄────► │    Secure login     │
│  Database   │        │   Queries   │        │  Automated Reports  │
│             │        │             │        │   Export & Share    │
└─────────────┘        └─────────────┘        └─────────────────────┘
```

The System Integration Protocols

As indicated above, the LEAP system requires the development of a set of protocols that guide the process of identifying learner analytics data which can subsequently inform faculty staff. Avondale has, for a number of years, operated a Virtual Mentor Program (VMP) aimed at identifying and, consequently, assisting students who were experiencing problems. The person in the Virtual Mentor (VM) role was employed on a part-time basis. The role involved monitoring students' progress and making contact with those students who appeared to be experiencing problems. When a student failed an assessment item, or did not engage with LMS activities, the VM contacted the student (usually by email, infrequently by phone) and noted the student's lack of progress. The VM was responsible for:

- monitoring students' progress by noting the grades a student obtained for their assessment items as they were recorded in each LMS Gradebook (a facility which stores the grades for each assessment item in the course students are enrolled);
- monitoring students' online engagement; tracking LMS engagement statistics allowed the VM to identify how often students accessed the LMS and which options they selected;
- contacting students who have failed an assessment item or had not participated in an online activity;
- maintaining subsequent and regular contact with at-risk students;
- tracking at-risk students across all the courses they were enrolled in;
- liaising with course coordinators and alerting them to problems their students were experiencing;
- keeping records of tracked student activities;
- analysing records and providing feedback about trends to the

Faculty and Program Convenors;
- identifying best practice to support students during their first year at university;
- facilitating student-staff relationships; and
- raising the visibility of at-risk or failing students.

Automating the VMP protocols in LEAP

The existing VMP utilizes a number of protocols to measure students' progress and students' levels of engagement for the purpose of identifying students who were exhibiting signs of disengagement or failing. The LEAP system utilized the lessons learned from the VMP, especially the engagement indicators which were used to track students' engagement levels. The lessons learned from the VMP informed the development of protocols within the LEAP system which made information about student engagement available to teachers. These protocols, referred to as engagement indicators in the VMP, included:

1. Access to LMS before the end of Week 2.
2. Downloaded "Course Outline" document before the end of Week 2.
3. Download additional "Student Information" booklet before the end of Week 3.
4. Access "News Forum" (course announcements) before the end of Week 3.
5. Frequency of access during Weeks 4-6.
6. Click count during Weeks 4-6.
7. Submission of Assessment Task 1 (and, if relevant, extension request).
8. Submission of Assessment Task 2 (and, if relevant, extension request).
9. Submission of Assessment Task 3 (and, if relevant, extension request).

Through the process of monitoring these activities, the VM was quickly able to identify students who were not performing to the expected standards or who demonstrated signs of failure. The VM followed a pre-determined process that ensured each student was treated equitably. The VM would send an informal message to any student who failed to achieve any of the engagement indicators.

The aim of this current project is to develop an automated approach, making students' progress transparent to academics through the application of the LEAP system through harnessing the latent data in the LMS, which were so successfully used in the manual processes in the VMP. Avondale is now aiming to provide teachers with 'live' data that reports on their students' performance against the engagement indicators. Avondale, with the Mobile Learning Company, will utilize the engagement indicators used in the VMP, to inform the extraction of relevant data from the LMS. The extraction of these data enables a report to be provided to each faculty member through a dashboard.

Results

Over the past few years, the VM project has worked well and has been proven to support students who were experiencing difficulty. However, it was very labour-intensive and limited in scope. Despite this, the benefits far outweighed the negative aspects of that program. The institution's current plan is to utilize the proven protocols, as used in the VMP, for identifying levels of student engagement, by incorporating them into the LEAP system which utilizes automation of the data in the LMS and makes these data, and the analysis of them, accessible to class teachers.

As an example of how the indicators present themselves in the classroom, student engagement levels were monitored as indicators and predictors of future success, as had been done in other studies (Atherton, Shah, Vazquez, Griffiths, Jackson, & Burgess, 2017; Saqr, Fors, & Tedre, 2017). Before the LEAP system was implemented, a class was monitored, manually, through the LMS, to look at how many times students were viewing their subject material, engaging with the activities, and accessing online resources on their LMS course site. This was simply measured by student "click counts" or views of LMS pages. Clicks were recorded over two periods during the semester: during Weeks 1-5 and Weeks 6-13. Figure 5.3 displays the relationship between the number of LMS views during those two periods and compares these with the total number of views for the semester with the final achieved grade.

Figure 5.3 Comparison of number of learning
management system (LMS) views with grades achieved

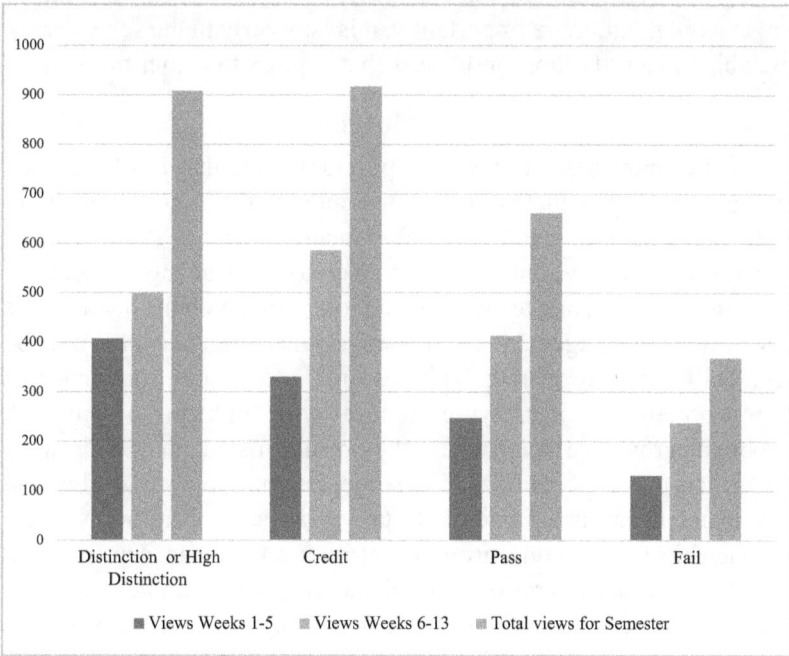

It is evident that there is a relationship between the number of clicks made by students in their LMS in Week 5 of the semester with their success or failure. Students with less than 200 clicks during the first five weeks of the semester invariably failed the class. At the Week 5 point in the semester, this is evident but it could be postulated that this would be evident at Week 2; this issue requires further study. Because these data about students' engagement, or non-engagement, in the first few weeks of the semester currently exists in the LMS, this project will provide ready access to such data for additional future investigations.

Scholarly Significance

The purpose of the project is to gain data defined by the engagement indicator protocols and bring them together in a dashboard which will present all the data in an easily understood form for the teachers to monitor the level of their students' engagement for the purpose of identifying students who are displaying problems in their studies, so early intervention is possible. The initial reports we have developed show that there is data of significance emerging which is giving us insight into our students' level of engagement with what we are teaching; but, more importantly, it is how early in the semester we are able to identify those indicators that appears to matter most.

Conclusion

This chapter has outlined two programs, one that has been used in the past and one that is under development. Both programs aim to decrease student attrition and, subsequently, increase student retention through empowering teachers to monitor student engagement. By using locally available technological tools, along with the institution's LMS, student engagement and non-engagement indicators are tracked to identify students at risk. This research adds to our knowledge of the importance of identifying students with problems before such problems grow to a point where they result in students withdrawing from their university studies. The strategies and programs outlined in this chapter may be of interest to university administrators who are responsible for arresting growing attrition rates or academic teaching staff who are interested in implementing some simple strategies, using an institution's LMS, to identify and support students at-risk.

Anthony Williams

Anthony Williams recently joined the University of Wollongong Global Enterprises Unit. The unit manages universities and colleges in four locations in Wollongong, Dubai, Hong Kong and Malaysia. Anthony manages the Academic Governance and Performance Portfolio across the institutions. Before taking up the Wollongong assignment, he was at Avondale where he was Vice President (Academic and Research) of Avondale College of Higher Education. He provided leadership in research and scholarship. Prior to that role, he held the position of the Head of School of Architecture and Built Environment at the University of Newcastle NSW. He has extensive experience in project management in the domain of professional education. He is a winner of multiple University Teaching Awards as well as a National Award for Teaching Excellence. He is highly regarded in this area having worked as a curriculum consultant nationally and internationally.

Maria Northcote

Maria Northcote is the Director of the Centre for Advancement of the Scholarship of Teaching and Learning (CASTL) at Avondale College of Higher Education. Maria is an experienced higher education teacher, leader and researcher and has successfully led an Office for Learning and Teaching Extension Grant through to completion during 2014-2015, and is currently a co-researcher on an Office for Learning and Teaching Seed Grant focusing on higher education assessment. She has led and contributed to a range of research projects in three higher education institutions between 1999 and 2015. Before beginning her work at Avondale, she worked at Newcastle and Edith Cowan Universities, in lecturing, research and staff development roles. She was recently appointed a Fellow of the Higher Education Research and Development Society of Australasia (HERDSA) in recognition of her service to higher education and her commitment to ongoing professional development to enhance teaching and learning.

John Reddin

John Reddin is a digital products and media professional with over 25 years of experience in production, product and service executive management roles. John has worked for and partnered with a range of enterprises from media, entertainment and technology companies like Google, Apple, Foxtel, YouTube, Amazon, BBC, and Sony, and with clients that range from major performing artists, artist management companies, and record labels, through to manufacturing and consumer brands. John is a co-founder and Director of Operations for mobileLearning.io, providing innovative mobile solutions to higher education institutions and public and private enterprises.

References

Atherton, M., Shah, M., Vazquez, J., Griffiths, Z., Jackson, B., & Burgess, C. (2017). Using learning analytics to assess student engagement and academic outcomes in open access enabling programmes. *Open Learning: The Journal of Open, Distance, and e-Learning, 32*(2), 119-136.

Booth, M. (2012). Learning analytics: The new black. *Educause Review, 47*(4). http://er.educause.edu/ articles/2012/7/learning-analytics-the-new-black

Bradley, D., Noonan, P., Nugent, H., & Scales, B. (2008). *Review of Australian higher education: Final report.* Canberra, Australia: Department of Education, Employment and Workplace Relations.

Kift, S. (2015). A decade of Transition Pedagogy: A quantum leap in conceptualising the first year experience. *HERDSA Review of Higher Education, 2*, 51-86.

Konstantinidis, A., & Grafton, C. (2013). Using Excel macros to analyse Moodle logs. *Proceedings of 2nd Moodle Research Conference* (pp. 33-39). Sousse, Tunisia.

Krause, K. L. (2005). The changing face of the first year: Challenges for policy and practice in research-led universities. Paper presented at the First Year Experience Workshop.

Krause, K. L., Hartley, R., James, R., & McInnis, C. (2005). *The first year experience in Australian universities: Findings from a decade of national studies.* Barton, Australia: Commonwealth of Australia, Department of Education, Science and Training.

Macfadyen, L. P., & Dawson, S. (2010). Mining LMS data to develop an "early warning system" for educators: A proof of concept. *Computers & Education, 54*(2), 588-599.

Masika, R., & Jones, J. (2016). Building student belonging and engagement: Insights into higher education students' experiences of participating and learning together. *Teaching in Higher Education, 21*(2), 138-150.

McInnis, C., Hartley, R., Polesel, J., & Teese, R. (2000). Non-completion in vocational education and training and higher education. Melbourne, Australia: Centre for the Study of Higher Education, The University of Melbourne & The Department of Education Training and Youth Affairs.

McInnis, C., James, R., & Hartley, R. (2000). *Trends in the first year experience: In Australian universities.* Canberra, Australia: Department of Education, Training and Youth Affairs Canberra.

Morris, L. V., Finnegan, C., & Wu, S. S. (2005). Tracking student behavior, persistence, and achievement in online courses. *The Internet and Higher Education, 8*(3), 221-231.

Pitkethly, A., & Prosser, M. (2001). The first year experience project: A model for university-wide change. *Higher Education Research & Development, 20*(2), 185-198.

Saqr, M., Fors, U., & Tedre, M. (2017). How learning analytics can early predict under-achieving students in a blended medical education course. *Medical Teacher*, 1-11.

Tinto, V. (1987). Leaving college: Rethinking the causes and cures of student attrition. Chicago, IL: The University of Chicago Press.

Tinto, V. (1999). Taking retention seriously: Rethinking the first year of college. *NACADA journal, 19*(2), 5-9.

Tinto, V., & Goodsell-Love, A. (1993). Building community. *Liberal Education, 79*(4), 16-22.

Yorke, M. (2000). The quality of the student experience: What can institutions learn from data relating to non-completion? *Quality in Higher Education, 6*(1), 61-75.

Zhao, C.-M., & Kuh, G. D. (2004). Adding value: Learning communities and student engagement. *Research in Higher Education, 45*(2), 115-138.

6. Getting on the Online Education Train: The Journey of a Small Higher Education Institution

Anthony Williams. Director of Academic Governance and Performance, The University of Wollongong Global Enterprises, Wollongong, Australia. Adjunct Professor, Avondale College of Higher Education, Cooranbong, Australia.

Maria Northcote. Associate Professor and Director of the Centre for Advancement of the Scholarship of Teaching and Learning. Avondale College of Higher Education

Abstract

Many universities have instituted professional learning centres that support academic teaching staff in their capacity to facilitate student-centred learning. Some of these centres also extend their reach to incorporate scholarship and research. This chapter reports on one such case, in which a small higher education institution in Australia established what has become known as the Centre for Advancement of the Scholarship of Teaching and Learning (CASTL). From its inception, the CASTL's intentions have been multidimensional, in that its programs, activities, and resource development span the following areas of scholarship: 1) learning and teaching, 2) researcher education and support of postgraduate supervision, and 3) the teaching-research nexus. This chapter outlines the research-informed processes adopted to design and develop the CASTL, and reports on some of the results that have been achieved since the establishment of this centre of scholarship.

Purpose

Avondale College of Higher Education was established in 1897 with a history representing 120 years of providing workers for the Seventh-day Adventist Church and for the broader community. The College's focus has been on teaching and, until recently, this has been face-to-face teaching only. In recent times, the College has changed this focus to encompass a wider range of teaching modes for two reasons: firstly, to increase its footprint across Australia and the

South Pacific region through the application of online learning; and secondly, there has been a significant emphasis within the College placed on blended learning, where the shift to a more student-centred approach to learning entails the use of both face-to-face and online learning approaches. Though the focus of this chapter is on the support for online education, it is important to understand that the boundary between online and face-to-face mode has blurred significantly in recent times.

The ability of Avondale to attract students from a broader community by offering online courses, instead of only concentrating on students who can attend the College physically, is a positive approach from the perspective of gaining more students, but there is a more important aim associated with this new focus. There are many students across Australia and the region who are not able to relocate to take up full-time study at the College in New South Wales. Furthermore, many people decide to change their career once they have established a family, and this is often the case with aspirational ministers, chaplains, and teachers who make up much of the institution's student population. The prospect of people in such circumstances being able to take three to four years out of their paid careers to study full-time is not always possible. So the opportunity to study part-time without relocating is of great advantage to these students who are typically in the mid-stage of their career and may also have a family to support. Studying online instead of attending classes in a face-to-face mode also allows students with a passion for such ministries as teaching and theology to take these careers up whilst funding their studies from their existing career. It goes without saying that many of these people, because of their life experience, make excellent teachers and ministers.

In recent decades, the College's distance education approach has involved a paper-based mode of instruction, often supported by lengthy on-campus summer school sessions with intensive class sessions or winter school sessions requiring students to travel to the College for one or two weeks for the purpose of engaging in intensive learning experiences. The paper-based distance learning mode was very restrictive in how it was able to engage students as it predominantly relied on textual materials which were sometimes supported by audiotapes. This approach is limited in the way it engages students and the College has been going through a transition to move toward more online education and less paper-based modes of study which have often required intensive on-campus teaching sessions.

A second consideration is that of blended learning; the potential for blended learning to provide students with an enhanced learning experience is well documented and Avondale sees the opportunity for improving the quality of its teaching and increasing accessibility to students through the medium of blended learning as great benefits. It is possible to sustain student learning outside of the face-to-face classroom through the application of blended learning. The ability to continue the learning into students' out-of-class time through online communication tools provides students with an enhanced learning experience as it sustains their learning, in a guided manner, through the whole week rather than just confining it to the three hours that is typically assigned for on-campus learning in face-to-face modes of study.

With these two purposes in mind Avondale has, over the past four years, focused a great deal of energy and effort into enhancing its online teaching and learning profile. Historically the focus has been on face-to-face teaching, with the advantage of having very small class sizes, but the College has started to broaden its horizons through the adoption of online education.

Theoretical Framework

Enabling academic teaching staff to make the transition to new modes of instruction requires considerable resources. Firstly, providing teaching staff with the technical or IT facilities to teach online is essential. Secondly, and perhaps more importantly, such staff also require support to develop their abilities to design and create appropriate teaching resources, the design of which needs to be informed by established principles drawn from the theories of online instructional design (Gunawardena et al., 2006; Herrington & Oliver, 2000; Siragusa, 2006). This need for course development skills also extends to the postgraduate coursework curriculum design. Instructional materials for higher degree and postgraduate students need to be developed with threshold concepts and the specific needs of postgraduate education in mind (Kiley, 2009; Meyer & Land, 2005; Wisker, Kiley, & Aiston, 2006).

The College is moving towards employing strategies and creating resources which are consistent with the learner-driven, self-directional theory of heutagogy (Hase & Kenyon, 2003). In additional to the coursework and supervisor-student sessions that are part of typical postgraduate courses, self-help resources, in the form of online modules, are also made available for postgraduate students on an 'as needed' basis. These self-help resources are consistent with Hase and Kenyon's (2003) principles of heutagogy, providing *just-in-time* support while also supporting *just-in-case* training activities. The concept is designed around the belief that an approach that "recognizes that people learn when they are ready and that this is most likely to occur quite randomly, chaotically, and in the face of ambiguity and need" (pp. 3-4), again frequently evidenced with postgraduate coursework students. According to heutagogical principles, learning resources can be provided by the teacher or selected for use by students as learning pathways are ultimately chosen by the learners themselves. These principles were integrated into the design of the developed resources.

This approach is most appropriate in the context of postgraduate research students where, under the guidance of their research supervisors, the students develop as independent researchers and acquire the knowledge, skills and attitudes required to conduct ethical research. Subsequently, because of the designed learning context of a community of practice, supervised postgraduate students can quickly transition to supervision of their own students (Morris, Pitt, & Manathunga, 2012). This dynamic process, developed between each postgraduate student and their supervision team, requires an approach to online learning that maximizes the flexibility afforded by a heutagogy-informed methodology.

The bringing together of the above approaches and strategies into a strategic approach has led to the successful development of a professional learning unit, that not only transcends practical approaches to teaching in online contexts but also covers the full range of teaching required in the Australian required academe, including undergraduate teaching, postgraduate coursework teaching, research training of postgraduate research students, and developing faculty members' research capacities. The initiative is broader in scope than equivalent centres but is also research-based. Following is an outline of the implementation of what has become a very successful centre, which aims to facilitate the development of an effective community of practice within the College.

Research Methodology

Essentially, the establishment of the Centre for Advancement of the Scholarship of Teaching and Learning (CASTL) within Avondale was driven by the institution's strategic long-term plan, as well as by the current and projected needs of its academic staff and students (both undergraduate and postgraduate). As the College is transitioning from an educational institution that had been characterized primarily for its undergraduate offerings to one that has now advanced into postgraduate education, the support offered to staff and students needs to traverse both course levels. The method by which the CASTL was established required a participatory approach that engaged as many stakeholders as possible, the stakeholders being the academic staff (teaching staff and postgraduate supervisors), the administration leadership team, as well as the institution's students. The outcome of this approach ensured that the establishment of the centre was built upon the needs of the faculty it aimed to support. As such, the academic community of the College became the participants in the research project which pre-empted the creation of the CASTL. As well as drawing on the views and needs of the College's staff and students, the way in which the CASTL was constructed also required consideration of the institution's strategic goals and a consideration of best practices in professional development, as reported in scholarly literature.

At the time when the CASTL was established, the institution was conducting a number of research projects which were focused on threshold concepts of online learning, innovative assessment feedback strategies, and the development of a researcher education framework. The ongoing data gathering methods that were embedded in these projects enabled localized information to be gathered from the CASTL's intended stakeholders about their professional development needs as well as expert advice from a number of reference groups. This information shaped the development of the CASTL's resources. Data were gathered from the following stakeholder-participants using a range of questionnaires, interviews, reflective journals, and focus groups:

- 60 academic staff and postgraduate supervisors;
- 12 postgraduate students;
- 44 undergraduate students; and
- 8 reference group members.

As a result, the CASTL's work within the institution was bounded by scholarly terms of reference ranging from learning and teaching support, through to researcher- and supervisor-education. All of these levels of support were underpinned by the teaching-research nexus in which teaching and learning activities were informed by research and, conversely, research was informed by teaching and learning issues relevant to the institution and its stakeholders. Each foray into the design and development of the Centre's programs was firstly driven by a need to analyse stakeholders' current positions and their projected future requirements and, secondly, the wider context of global research. The institution's vision and strategic goals were used as additional input and incorporated into the Centre's vision statement, programs, and activities.

Once established in March 2015, the Centre used a form of Patton's (2012) utilisation-focused evaluation methodology to develop its programs, activities, and supporting resources. This approach enabled heuristic (Hase, 2014; Hase & Kenyon, 2015) principles of learning, incorporating self-determined and capacity-building strategies which were embedded in the work of CASTL staff. For example, rather than simply designing a professional learning program that was informed by best practice literature about online education to assist academic staff to develop their capacities as online course designers and teachers, the actual staff for whom the program was being developed were consulted. It was their views, along with experts' considerations cited in current scholarly literature, which determined the nature and content of the program that was ultimately developed to meet their needs. Data about their needs were gathered within the confines of a scholarly research project about online teaching, supported by a Seed Grant through a key government-funded initiative at the time, The Office for Learning and Teaching in Australia. Other examples of the outcomes of establishing the CASTL are now presented.

Results

As a result of establishing a centre of scholarship, Avondale was then in a position to move towards designing and developing professional learning programs, activities, events, and resources. A selection of these outcomes is now described and presented as the results of the establishment of the CASTL.

Because the Centre was so focused on integrating the three areas of research, learning, and teaching, the research projects it supported were related to these concerns. While also tending to the needs of academic staff and students within the institution, the CASTL's research projects were situated within a national educational context by attracting key government funding through Australia's Office for Learning and Teaching. Since 2014, the College was successful in gaining four of these sought-after grants across three funding programs, including: two Seed Grants (AU$40,000 and AU$50,000), one Extension Grant of AU$29,800, and one Innovation and Development Grant of AU$202,000. The titles of the grants, listed below, reflect their diverse nature and indicate how they spanned undergraduate and postgraduate education, while also addressing issues incorporating students' and teachers' concerns:

1. Using online teaching threshold concepts in transformative professional learning curricula for novice online educators.
2. But when do I get my mark? Students' responsiveness to adaptively released assessment feedback.
3. Developing an institutional framework to support and improve supervision of honours and higher degree research students.
4. Owning the rubric: Student engagement in rubric design, use, and moderation.

The implementation of these scholarly research projects resulted in the growing reputation of the CASTL's work within the institution as well as across the higher education sector. Since its launch, the Centre's staff have collaborated with many national and international scholars from over 19 national universities and 9 international universities on a number of programs, including:

- Visiting scholar program in which 7 national and 4 international scholars have visited and/or resided at Avondale for short stays of a few days through to longer stays of up to five months.
- Virtual Mentoring Program in which first year students' progress was monitored and supported by a Virtual Mentor (now transitioning to LEAP, as mentioned in Chapter 5).
- Evaluation of Avondale's distance education program in conjunction with one of our international collaborating researchers.
- Co-editing of a scholarly international handbook of research (complete) and a set of refereed proceedings for an international learning conference (underway).

While many of the outcomes of the projects conducted through the CASTL have resulted in immediate benefits for staff and students in the form of the programs listed above, some outcomes are of an ongoing nature: many projects have produced self-paced or self-help style scholarly resources, including:

Research Training Support Framework, available at: http://www. avondale.edu.au/research-training. This resource provides support, advice, and resources for Avondale staff involved in the supervision of honours and postgraduate students, and candidates enrolled in honours and postgraduate research degrees.

Transformational Assessment Toolbox, available at: http://assessment.avondale.edu.au/toolboxtat. This online toolbox has been designed especially for use within the higher education sector and may be of particular interest to course designers and lecturers who are interested in rethinking traditional processes of providing assessment feedback to their students with the intention of engaging students in reflection about their own learning by transforming some elements of the assessment process.

Threshold Concepts for Novice Online Teachers site, available at: http://tcs4nots.avondale.edu.au. This site features curriculum guidelines to inform the design of transformative professional development for novice online educators, along with the findings of the project.

Other materials produced by CASTL staff include in-house, homegrown resources that provide self-help assistance by offering best practice examples, technical instructions, suggestions for professional learning activities, and links to external resources. Some of these homegrown resources include: *The Researcher's Little Helper* (https://moodle.avondale.edu.au/login/index.php), *Moodle's Little Helper* (http://moodle.avondale.edu.au/course/view.php?id=1317), *Assessment @ Avondale* (http://assessment.avondale.edu.au); the *MOOBRIC* (http://www.moobric.net/) and a selection of online instructional modules that support the professional learning of research students, postgraduate supervisors, and undergraduate teachers.

In addition to research projects and the development of scholarly programs and resources, the CASTL has also facilitated a range of on-campus and online events that support the scholarly integration of research and teaching, and/or the scholarly development of learning and teaching capacities. Some of these recent events include:

- panel discussion to brainstorm current needs[1] of academic teaching and research staff;

---

[1]   Some of the current needs identified during this consultation session included: access to online professional development modules, permanent agenda item in faculty meetings to advertise CASTL events, and collation of all professional learning resources on one website.

- drop-in sessions to provide advice about the use of online learning management systems;
- showcases of what works and doesn't work in online education;
- informal researcher lunches;
- grant writing circles;
- speed-dating with researchers to share research topics, ideas, and methodologies;
- networking morning teas for research students and their postgraduate supervisors; and
- interviews with visiting scholars.

These strategic initiatives are presented here in this chapter as results of the CASTL's work. These programs, activities, and resources are examples of how scholarship was integrated into learning and teaching, by supporting scholarly research and, conversely, encouraging the incorporation of recent research into learning and teaching activities. The overlapping of ideas, models, and practices between faculties within the institution, as well as between visiting scholars and Avondale's academic staff, shape the success of Avondale's scholarship focus and ongoing development.

The CASTL's programs, activities and resources undergo regular evaluation, the results of which have been or are being reported elsewhere (for example, Petrie et al., 2016). The evaluation methodologies used to assess the impact and effectiveness of these initiatives have adopted a mixture of utilisation-focused evaluation methodologies (Patton, 2012, 2015) and design-based research methodologies (Anderson & Shattuck, 2012; Kennedy-Clark, 2013).

Scholarly Significance

It is difficult to describe the diversity of activity in a research and teaching higher education context; diversity is represented in varied teaching initiatives, assessment, and engaged learning practices, as well as varied types of student centred, online, blended, and authentic approaches. All are worthy agendas for a scholarship Centre, but these agendas are far from the limits of the Centre's full scope. It was always envisaged that the College would need to assist in the development of a research culture. This is a new area of focus for the College, something that typically takes universities many years to develop. A university's research culture ideally covers the two aspects of research training: the support of postgraduate research students undertaking PhDs as well as the provision of professional learning experiences for academic staff to develop research skills and abilities. The CASTL has effectively provided these two aspects of research training. Furthermore, the number of competitive grants won by the institution is evidence of such training. The College's research profile continues to extend, with significant growth in research enrolments and completions, as well as a bourgeoning publication profile which reflected 400% growth between 2012 and 2014 with 763 submissions made to the ResearchOnline@Avondale (http://research.avondale.edu.au/) repository between 2012 and 2014[2].

The establishment of a community of practice amongst many of the staff augers well for the future. Academic staff at the College are now regularly collaborating on scholarly writing activities related to the innovations implemented in their teaching practice which, eventually, is shared in the form of research publications. The College has changed its singular profile of face-to-face teaching to a profile that now includes online learning, blended learning, research training, and research development. In doing so the College has become multidimensional and its scope continues to grow. Importantly, the CASTL has been the driver of this change and it continues to lead in the enhancement of both practice and scholarship.

Conclusion

This chapter has outlined how establishment of a centre for learning, teaching, and research has produced a set of scholarly results for a burgeoning higher education sector. By drawing on examples of best practice from scholarly literature as well as consulting with its stakeholders, including the institution's teaching staff and students, the results of the CASTL's work has been presented as a collection of programs, activities, and resources. These initiatives are characterized by an interrelationship between teaching, learning, and research: that is, scholarship that integrates research into all of its work. The participatory methods used to develop this centre of scholarship as well as the stakeholder-focused methodologies used to conduct and evaluate its activities and programs may be of interest to administrators and professional development staff in other higher education institu-

---

[2]   Data supplied on Friday 8 September 2017 by Avondale librarian responsible for Avondale's ResearchOnline repository (http://research.avondale.edu.au/).

tions, especially those who intend to provide professional learning opportunities that are not only useful for the present but provide an educational future that is pedagogically sustained by and grounded in scholarship.

Anthony Williams

Anthony Williams recently joined the University of Wollongong Global Enterprises Unit. The unit manages universities and colleges in four locations in Wollongong, Dubai, Hong Kong and Malaysia. Anthony manages the Academic Governance and Performance Portfolio across the institutions. Before taking up the Wollongong assignment, he was at Avondale where he was Vice President (Academic and Research) of Avondale College of Higher Education. He provided leadership in research and scholarship. Prior to that role, he held the position of the Head of School of Architecture and Built Environment at the University of Newcastle NSW. He has extensive experience in project management in the domain of professional education. He is a winner of multiple University Teaching Awards as well as a National Award for Teaching Excellence. He is highly regarded in this area having worked as a curriculum consultant nationally and internationally.

Maria Northcote

Maria Northcote is the Director of the Centre for Advancement of the Scholarship of Teaching and Learning (CASTL) at Avondale College of Higher Education. Maria is an experienced higher education teacher, leader and researcher and has successfully led an Office for Learning and Teaching Extension Grant through to completion during 2014-2015, and is currently a co-researcher on an Office for Learning and Teaching Seed Grant focusing on higher education assessment. She has led and contributed to a range of research projects in three higher education institutions between 1999 and 2015. Before beginning her work at Avondale, she worked at Newcastle and Edith Cowan Universities, in lecturing, research and staff development roles. She was recently appointed a Fellow of the Higher Education Research and Development Society of Australasia (HERDSA) in recognition of her service to higher education and her commitment to ongoing professional development to enhance teaching and learning.

References

Anderson, T., & Shattuck, J. (2012). Design-based research: A decade of progress in education research? *Educational Researcher, 41*(1), 16-25.

Gunawardena, C. N., Ortegano-Layne, L., Carabajal, K., Frechette, C., Lindemann, K., & Jennings, B. (2006). New model, new strategies: Instructional design for building online wisdom communities. *Distance Education, 27*(2), 217-232.

Hase, S. (2014). Heutagogy and e-learning in the workplace: Some challenges and opportunities. *Impact: Journal of Applied Research in Workplace E-learning, 1*(1), 43-52.

Hase, S., & Kenyon, C. (2003, 25-27 September). *Heutagogy and developing capable people and capable workplaces: Strategies for dealing with complexity.* Paper presented at the Proceedings of The Changing Face of Work and Learning Conference, Alberta, Canada.

Hase, S., & Kenyon, C. (2015). *Self-determined learning: Heutagogy in action.* London: Bloomsbury Academic.

Herrington, J., & Oliver, R. (2000). An instructional design framework for authentic learning environments *Journal Educational Technology Research and Development, 48*(3), 23-48.

Kennedy-Clark, S. (2013). Research by design: Design-based research and the higher degree research student. *Journal of Learning Design, 6*(26-32). Retrieved from https://www.jld.edu.au/ article/view/257

Kiley, M. (2009). Identifying threshold concepts and proposing strategies to support doctoral candidates. *Innovations in Education and Teaching International, 46*(3), 293-304.

Meyer, J. H. F., & Land, R. (2005). Threshold concepts and troublesome knowledge (2): Epistemological considerations and a conceptual framework for teaching and learning. *Higher Education, 49*(3), 373–388.

Morris, S., Pitt, R., & Manathunga, C. (2012). Students' experiences of supervision in academic and industry settings: Results of an Australian study. *Assessment & Evaluation in Higher Education, 37*(5), 619-636.

Patton, M. Q. (2012). A utilization-focused approach to contribution analysis. *Evaluation, 18*(3), 364-377. doi:10.1177/1356389012449523

Patton, M. Q. (2015). *Qualitative research and evaluation methods* (4th ed.). Thousand Oaks, California: SAGE Publications, Inc.

Petrie, K., Anderson, M., de Waal, K., Mitchell, B. G., Northcote, M., Williams, A., & Carton, J. (2016). Designing an innovative system to evaluate a postgraduate supervision support and development framework. In M. Picard & A. McCulloch (Eds.), *Proceedings of the 12th Biennial Quality in Postgraduate Research Conference: Society, Economy & Communities: 21st Century innovation in Doctoral Education* (pp. 132-138). Adelaide, South Australia: University of Adelaide, University of South Australia and Flinders University.

Siragusa, L. (2006). *Quality eLearning: An instructional design model for online learning in higher education.* Paper presented at the Annual Conference of Australian Association for Research in Education, Adelaide.

Wisker, G., Kiley, M., & Aiston, S. (2006). Making the learning leap: Research students crossing conceptual thresholds In M. Kiley & G. Mullines (Eds.), *Quality in postgraduate research: Knowledge creation in testing times.* Canberra: CEDAM, The Australian National University.

Collaboration

In the tradition of the Adventist Virtual Learning Network, we cannot consider online education and technology-enhanced teaching without considering ways to use technology to collaborate. Technological tools have the potential to break down barriers and make it easier to collaborate across schools, institutions, even generations. Carolina Costa Cavalcanti, Everson Muckenberger, and Andrea Filatro explore a unique strategy of reverse coaching with young mentoring the more mature, and the senior leaders mentoring the junior leaders. Robert Paulson and Shirley Freed share results of research on the readiness of faculty and administrators for interinstitutional collaboration.

7. Reverse Coaching In Online Corporate Education

Carolina Costa Cavalcanti. Professor. Adventist University of São Paulo (UNASP). Corresponding Author: carolina.cavalcanti@ucb.org.br

Everson Muckenberger. Academic Manager. Adventist University of São Paulo (UNASP)

Andrea Filatro. Speaker, author and researcher in Instructional Design. Adventist University of São Paulo (UNASP)

Abstract

This study investigates the adoption of reverse coaching as a strategy to promote the involvement of different generations in an online course to train leaders. Young people acted as technology coaches for older adults with less digital fluency. On the other hand, senior leaders, with greater experience and leadership skills, acted as coaches for young potential leaders. Among the objectives of the course, senior leaders and young potential leaders were expected to learn how to lead younger generations, a topic discussed and practiced during the course in the study unit entitled "Relevant Leadership for New Generations," which reinforced the practice and justified the adoption of reverse coaching in the leadership course. The pilot group investigated was composed of 280 participants distributed in five geographic regions of Brazil. Through the analysis of frequency, correspondence analysis, and comparison of medians, it was verified that reverse coaching is associated positively with participation/performance and course completion that led to student certification.

Introduction and Objectives

Reverse coaching is a relatively new methodology for conducting corporate education actions and motivating adults to exchange knowledge and develop skills in a collaborative way. This methodology has been applied with or without the use of technology, for example, with groups of students with competencies from different areas, but it has been successfully used to integrate people from different generations.

For instance, Barraclough et al. (2012) and Baily (2009) indicate that many companies have used reverse coaching by pairing young people (Millennials) to help older employees (Boomers) on technology skills, to understand the mind-sets that guide the actions of new generations and to be open to learn new things. On the other hand, adults with greater experience within a certain knowledge or professional area can act as coaches for young beginners (Chaudhuri & Ghosh, 2012).

This chapter investigates reverse coaching as a strategy to promote the involvement of different generations in an online course that aims to train leaders. To verify the effectiveness of the methodology, we present the instructional design proposal, the technological resources employed, and the results achieved, in order to verify the correlation between reverse coaching and the results of the online course student's participation/performance and certification.

Theoretical Foundation

Corporate education can be defined as a professional educational system based on people management, whose focus is the development of the internal (collaborators/employees) and external (clients, family, distributors, suppliers, partners, among others) publics of an organization. Eboli (2012) indicates that corporate education aims to develop fundamental skills to enable the organization's business strategies, through the adoption of an active learning process that is linked to purposes, objectives, and goals established by the company.

Corporate education has several similarities to regular or traditional education. Companies, non-profit institutions, and public and private organizations responsible for training people, have adopted corporate education to stimulate the dissemination of the organizational culture and to update the knowledge of their collaborators.

Access to information and communication technologies opened new possibilities to meet the demands of organizations. Thus, online education has been incorporated into corporate education through the implementation of courses and programs that aim at developing specific skills, within specific groups of people, through individual or collaborative learning (Ferreira, Valério, & Souza, 2010).

In fact, online education presents advantages over face-to-face professional training programs such as: the ease of reaching large numbers of employees, the agility to disseminate and share knowledge and information, the possibility of reproducing and updating the contents produced, and provision of activities to be carried out individually and collaboratively (Eboli, 2012). Some limitations of the model are: the feeling of isolation of the online student, the difficulty in using technology, and, depending on the pedagogical model adopted, the absence of collaborative learning (Ferreira, Valério, & Souza, 2010).

Collaborative learning assumes that the collective construction of knowledge occurs only through social interaction (Vygotsky, 1987). Nowadays, the abilities to work in groups, to learn with one another, and to co-create are fundamental for a professional in the job market (Cavalcanti, 2012). This type of learning is valued in corporate education as it prepares employees to solve problems and conflicts, leads them to share and generate new ideas, and encourages them to build knowledge collectively by networking in interdisciplinary teams.

The birth of reverse coaching can be traced to the reverse mentoring concept that was introduced in 1999 in General Electric by its CEO Jack Welch who wanted to create more meaningful and enduring learning experiences in corporate education contexts. At the company, new young employees were assigned to work in a long-term partnership with senior managers or employees, to teach them how to use the Internet. On the other hand, older workers helped young people to acquire knowledge and skills that should be applied in the workplace (Chaudhuri & Ghosh, 2012). Over time, other companies identified that young people had technological know-how, skills, and mind-sets that could be shared with senior employees and that the experience of senior managers and executives could be shared with younger collaborators (Baily, 2009; Chaudhuri & Ghosh, 2012).

A couple of years later, in corporate education environments where there was no time to establish a long-term relationship between a senior mentor and a young mentoree (as was done in reverse mentoring), the so-called **reverse coaching** was created and adopted with success (Ely et al., 2010). Reverse coaching was an unfolding of reverse mentoring that was characterized as a time-limited vocational training strategy that aimed at the knowledge exchange between individuals with different profiles and experiences (Ely et al., 2010). Reverse coaching commonly occurs among people of different generations or genders when it is recognized that people of varying ages and characteristics can interact for learning and teaching purposes, considering the point of view of others.

For example, Chaudhuri and Ghosh (2012) describe that Procter & Gamble created a program to help male managers understand the challenges young women face when joining the professional world. This and other experiences have made the practice of reverse coaching popular in corporate education. In many cases, young professionals are expected to teach senior employees to use technology resources and to see the world from a perspective that is aligned with the new generations' thoughts and wants. On the other hand, senior managers are expected to prepare and guide young employees to face daily workplace challenges and dilemmas, helping them to find answers to complex questions, such as: Is it possible to find a balance between career and personal life? How to face challenges in the professional world and draw lessons from the difficulties? (Baily, 2009; Chaudhuri & Ghosh, 2012; Ely et al., 2010).

Literature indicates that the use of strategies such as reverse coaching brings benefits to both young people and senior managers. Young employees feel supported and secure because they realize that the work they do is significant and relevant which brings tangible benefits to their career. At the same time, dealing with young people is beneficial to more experienced managers and collaborators, who end up developing skills in areas they did not master previously, while they learn how young people think, work, behave, and relate, which gives them benefits in their professional performance and worldview. These exchanges stimulate generational bridge building, which fosters social and cultural exchange, facilitating a significant learning process (Barraclough et al. 2012; Chaudhuri & Ghosh, 2012; Ely et al., 2010).

Researched Context

The **Leadership for Elders** course was designed to inspire, motivate, and empower leaders who act or will voluntarily work in an ecclesiastical environment. Elder is the designation given to the member of the church who voluntarily exercises spiritual leadership in the church, conducting the services and ministering in word and doctrine. The goal is to enable elders to exercise effective and meaningful leadership that positively influences their local community. The demand for this specific course came from the South American Division (SAD) of the Seventh-day Adventist (SDA) Church, which contracted with the Adventist University of São Paulo (UNASP) to develop an online course.

In Latin America, SAD manages 53 regional Conferences, which manage local churches spread across the continent. For more than 50 years, SAD has provided training courses for its contracted employees (such as pastors and teachers) and for volunteer church members and leaders in several areas such as theology, health, management, and music.

Online learning corporate education at SAD has been implemented recently as some online courses were offered to volunteer members and leaders. The Leadership for Elders course is one of the first initiatives and it targets an audience of 20,000 leaders and young future leaders in South America that will take the course in the next five years. The pilot course analyzed in this chapter was held in the second semester of 2016.

The leaders who make up the target audience of the course were elders of local small, medium, or large churches, with diverse formal educational background. From the 280 participants of the pilot online course, 49% completed higher education, 42% completed high school, and 9% completed only elementary school. In any case, to be an elder, these men have demonstrated leadership skills and have a good reputation in the inner and outer community. They are invited by the local conference to participate in the online course, offered free of charge, on a voluntary basis, with no compulsory approval or penalty if it is not completed. Differentiating this course from a MOOC (Massive Open Online Course), the Leadership for Elders course had one entry requirement: participants should be selected by the regional Conference.

The idea of adopting reverse coaching in this specific course emerged when the pedagogical team, formed by professionals with training in instructional design and education, carried out a previous study called "Contextual Analysis." Tessmer and Richey (1997) proposed this analysis, in order to capture the multidimensional approach of a learning context.[1] From the "Contextual Analysis" results, the pedagogical team understood the training demands.

---

[1] Basically, contextual analysis encompasses: a) orientation context: prior to learning, influences the future motivation of the student, and prepares him cognitively to learn; b) instructional context: usually determined temporarily by the instructional event (course, program, class), involves the physical, social, and symbolic resources that are part of the didactic situation; c) transfer context: after learning, it basically involves the environment or the situation in which learning will be applied. These three contexts express three different levels of comprehensiveness: a) the individual perspective, characteristic of the student; b) the immediate perspective, characteristic of the environment; c) the cultural or institutional perspective, characteristic of an organization, institution or society (Filatro, 2004).

Initially, SAD's request was to offer a course only to the leaders who were already elders in congregations located throughout South America. However, the contextual analysis indicated that two challenges existed: (1) many of the elders, especially those living in locations outside of large urban centers, were unfamiliar with the use of technology; 2) in a short time, it would be necessary to train new leaders to take on the activities of more experienced elders.

From this observation, the pedagogical team suggested the adoption of reverse coaching to help solve these two identified challenges: the use of technology by the most experienced leaders and the development of new leaders. However, due to the difficulty in ensuring that the leaders adhered to the course's reverse coaching proposal, it was decided that the participants could also carry out the online course activities individually, with the same possibility of completion and certification. Once the proposal was approved, the course was developed.

The pilot course analyzed in this chapter was composed of a total of 280 participants distributed in 5 geographic regions of Brazil. Participants were enrolled in the course in pairs made up of one experienced senior elder and a colleague, at least 10 years younger, digitally fluent, and a candidate to take over as a leader in the near future. Each experienced elder could select and appoint a younger leader in his local church or area to participate in the course in a collaborative way. The creation of pairs was not done randomly, but based on the experienced leader's indication of a young man who could one day assume his duties. During the introductory unit of the course, participants were advised on how to work in pairs to complete the proposed activities called "challenges."

The course was launched in a face-to-face opening class held in five Brazilian cities where the pilot was conducted. One of the four teachers who taught the course's online video lessons taught this face-to-face opening class. At this meeting, participants received a login and password to access the course's Virtual Learning Environment (VLE). It was also at that moment that participants were introduced to their online tutors who would guide them in the online-proposed activities. The course participants also received general information about the course structure and chronogram.

This online pilot course was organized into 6 weekly study units. Therefore, the leaders knew the period they had to complete the course

was between August and September 2016. The study units were orga-
nized as it follows:
- Introduction unit
- **Unit 1** - Biblical Leadership Principles
- **Unit 2** - Participatory Leadership
- **Unit 3** - Relevant Leadership for the New Generations
- **Unit 4** – Leadership for Disciples
- Closing Unit

In each study unit, participants had access to exclusive and interactive online video lessons, recorded by professors with a Masters
or PhD degree in the areas of theology and leadership. In addition,
they had access to digital contents (such as articles, e-books, slides,
videos) and activities (such as quizzes and challenges) that were to be
done individually or in pairs.

The **challenges** were special activities that aimed to connect the
content presented in the video lessons and texts with the reality of the
local church. The leaders were instructed to develop the challenges
in pairs, using the VLE (MoodleRooms) and social networks (such
as Facebook, Twitter, Instagram, and LinkedIn), and to collect data
in face-to-face activities in their communities. In some challenges,
leaders were invited to interview other leaders and members with different characteristics (young/old, single/married etc.) in their church
communities, in order to explore the potential of social networks in
leadership for the new generations and to learn about the elders' experiences in other churches.

Course participants were instructed to use technology and online
tools available in MoodleRooms (such as forums, internal mail, and
database activity) and resources from their phone (such as instant message and social media) to engage and communicate with their reverse
coaching pair. Even though most pairs were physically located in the
same city, and performed some activities in physical locations, such
as the church, all activities were proposed, recorded, and discussed in
the VLE, under the supervision of the online tutor.

Students received course completion certificates if they had
accessed the course materials and had submitted the proposed challenges for each study unit, in pairs or individually. In addition, to
receive the certificate, they were to answer an assessment questionnaire on their perceptions about the course, available for them in the
VLE (MoodleRooms).

Furthermore, a closing meeting, previously scheduled, was held in the five locations where the pilot course was applied; the participants could share positive and negative aspects of their online experience and suggest improvements for the course. Many of those who participated at the closing meeting reported that they did not receive the completion certificate, because they did not participate in some of the challenges. However, even so, they believed that it was very enriching to their volunteer ministry to participate in the course, to access the proposed contents, and to know the perspective of other leaders, portrayed in the online discussions.

Research Methodology

To test the hypothesis that reverse coaching had a significant impact on the participation/performance and certification of participants, data recorded in MoodleRooms were analyzed.

The variables used in the analysis were classified into context variables and outcome variables, as shown in Table 7.1.

Initially, the frequency distributions of the variables were analyzed. Then, through correspondence analysis, applying chi-square tests, the correlation between the context variables and outcome variables was investigated. Finally, participation/performance was compared between those who participated in reverse coaching and those who did not participate in the reverse coaching, through Mann-Whitney median comparison test.

Table 7.1 Variables used for Analysis

Context variables	**Profile**	Whether the participant was an elder or a young person.
	Coaching	Whether the participant was or was not engaged in a reverse coaching pair during the course, as originally proposed.
	Region	Region of the country where the participant resided.
Outcome variables	**Participation/ Performance**	Sum of student's accumulated score for each activity completed.
	Certification	Whether the participant had or had not fulfilled the necessary requirements to obtain the course completion certification.

Results and Discussion

From the analysis of the frequency distributions, it was possible to verify 280 leaders who actually participated in the course. Of these, 139 were senior leaders (elders) and 141 young leaders in training. The participation/performance of the students, represented by the sum of scores obtained in the activities completed, was quite diverse (Standard Deviation = 48.6), ranging from 0 to 160 points, with the mode at 20 points and the median at 80 points. Of the total number of participants who started the course, 31% were certified and 69% did not complete the course. As for reverse coaching, 23% of the participants worked in functional reverse coaching pairs, formed by a senior leader and a young leader in training, and 77% preferred not to adhere to the reverse coaching strategy.

In order to provide better criteria for analysis, the participation/performance variable was categorized into four scoring categories, according to Table 7.2.

Table 7.2 Distribution of Frequency of Scores in Categories

Categories	Freq.	%
Up to 30 points	84	30
From 31 to 80 points	65	23
From 81 to 120 points	72	26
More than 120 points	59	21
Total	280	100

At the crosstabs of context variables and outcome variables, the only context variable correlated significantly and positively with outcome variables was the reverse coaching adherence variable. The participants who engaged in reverse coaching pairs not only had a higher degree of certification in the course (Table 7.3) but also had higher scores (Table 7.4).

It is important to emphasize that all students who completed the course and were certified were in functional reverse coaching pairs. Inevitably, this finding raises the hypothesis that a greater commitment to reverse coaching also increased the certification rate among participants.

Table 7.3 Functionality of Reverse Coaching Pairs and Course Certification

Reverse Coaching Pairs	Certification		Total
	Certified	Not certified	
Functional	100%	0%	100%
Not functional	10%	90%	100%
% of total students	31%	69%	100%

Note. N = 280. Chi-square = 187,149; p = 0.000

Table 7.4 Functionality of Reverse Coaching Pairs and Achieved Scores

Reverse Coaching Pairs	Scores				Total
	Up to 30	31 to 80	81 to 120	More than 120	
Functional	0%	0%	31%	69%	100%
Not functional	39%	30%	24%	7%	100%
% of total students	30%	23%	26%	21%	100%

Note. N = 280. Chi-square = 134,640; p = 0.000.

Concerning performance scores, the total number of students engaged in reverse coaching pairs scored above average (mean = 80 points), while 69% of those not engaged in reverse coaching pairs scored below it. It is still relevant to note that 69% of the students engaged in reverse coaching pairs scored higher than 120 points, while only 7% of those not so engaged reached the same level.

When comparing engaged and non-engaged participants in reverse coaching pairs it was found that the score was significantly different (Mann-Whitney, $p = 0.000$) between these two groups. Therefore, the reverse coaching is not only positively associated with the participation/performance and certification, but also differentiates the participation/performance of the students.

No significant correlation was found between the student's profile, whether senior leader or young leader, and any of the outcome variables (Certification: Chi-square $= 0.192$, $p = 0.661$; Participation/Performance: Chi-square $= 0.201$, $p = 0.977$). There was also no distinction between the individual performance of senior leaders and that of the young leaders (Mann-Whitney, $p = 0.734$).

It is important to remember that reverse coaching was used for overcoming eventual technological barriers among senior leaders and the reduction of a possible lack of interest on the part of the young people in exerting voluntary leadership in the local church context. The non-significance of the profile variable, combined with the significance of the coaching variable on the outcome variables, suggests that these objectives were achieved, reinforcing Baily (2009), Barraclough et al. (2012), Chaudhuri and Ghosh (2012), and Ely et al., (2010), when they affirm that reverse coaching can bring benefits to all involved in contexts of corporate education (online or face-to-face).

Final Considerations

This study aimed to verify the correlation between reverse coaching and participation/performance and certification in the Leadership for Elders online pilot course, among senior leaders who volunteer as elders in an SDA church and younger leaders, in the second semester of 2016.

Results confirmed that reverse coaching is positively associated with participation/performance and certification for the pilot group analyzed. Data also showed that participants who engaged in reverse coaching pairs presented a higher degree of certification and higher performance/participation scores, when compared to those not engaged.

According to the analyzed data for the pilot online course, the pedagogical team reinforced the relevance of adopting reverse coaching in regular groups of this course starting from May 2017, thus aiming to reach more than three thousand leaders, distributed in all Brazilian states. After analyzing the pilot data, the pedagogical team also extended the course's introductory unit for two weeks, instead of one, so that the tutors may have sufficient time to prepare the pairs more appropriately, so they can adhere to the reverse coaching methodological proposal. It is expected that the participants' engagement will increase and, as a result, more volunteers will be approved and certificated.

For future implications, we can extend the methodology of reverse coaching to other institutional contexts. Reverse coaching could be used not only to promote exchange and mutual aid between groups with evident generational differences, but also between groups with different degrees of maturity or levels of competence, such as leaders of communication with music or sports volunteers, university graduates with field missionaries, parents with teachers of Sabbath School classes, among other fruitful combinations.

Carolina Costa Cavalcanti

Carolina Costa Cavalcanit is a professor, researcher, and author in the field of education. She earned a PhD in Education from the University of São Paulo/USP, in Brazil, a Master in Educational Technologies from the Monterrey Institute of Technology in Mexico, and her undergraduate degree in education from UNISA, Brazil. Carolina also has a degree in journalism from Southwestern Adventist University, USA. Currently she serves as the coordinator of the graduate program "Innovation and Design in Education" at the Adventist University of São Paulo (UNASP, Brazil).

Everson Muckenberger

Everson Muckenberger is the academic manager for online education at the Adventist University of São Paulo (UNASP, Brazil). He is a professor and researcher in business administration and organizational management. Everson holds a PhD in Organizational Management from the University of São Paulo, (USP), Brazil; a Master in Business Administration from the University of Rio Grande do Sul, (UFRGS) in Brazil, and a Bachelor in Business Administration from the University of Santa Catarina (UFSC), Brazil.

Andrea Filatro

Andrea Filatro is a speaker, author and researcher in instructional design. She earned a PhD and Masters in Education from the University of São Paulo (USP), Brazil. She holds a graduate degree in project management from the University of São Paulo (USP), Brazil. She serves as a consultant in online education in the academic and corporate sectors within Brazil and South America. In addition she is currently coordinator of educational design at the Adventist University of São Paulo (UNASP), Brazil.

References

Baily, C. (2009). Reverse intergenerational learning: A missed opportunity? *AI and Society, 23*(1), 111-115.

Barraclough, S., Claxton, J., Gaston, S., Glaister, C., Horsman, D., James, C., & Preece, D. (2012) *HRD in 2020: The era of the individual?* Paper submitted for the 'HRD in 2020', European HRD Conference, Portugal, 2012. Retrieved from http://www.ufhrd.co.uk/wordpress/wp-content/uploads/2012/ 11/UFHRD2012Future71.pdf

Cavalcanti, C. C. (2012) *Autoavaliação do trabalho colaborativo por projetos na formação de educadores a distância [Self-assessment of project collaborative work in distance learning for educators].* Anais do II Seminário Web Currículo – Educação e Mobilidade. São Paulo: PUC-SP.

Chaudhuri, S., & Ghosh, R. (2012). Reverse mentoring: A social exchange tool for keeping the boomers engaged and millennials committed. *Human Resource Development Review, 11*(1), 55-76.

Eboli, M. (2012). Sistema de educação corporativa e a EAD [Corporative education system and distance learning]. In: Litto, F. M., & Formiga, M. *Educação a distância: o estado da arte [Distance learning: the state of art].* São Paulo: Pearson Education do Brasil, v. 2.

Ely, K., Boyce, L. A., Nelson, J. K., Zaccaro, S. J., Hernez-Broome, G., & Whyman, W. (2010). Evaluating leadership coaching: A review and integrated framework. *The Leadership Quarterly, 28*(4), 585-599.

Ferreira, A., Valério, J. N. G., & Souza, G. C. (2010). A educação a distância nas organizações: A percepção sobre o e-learning em uma grande empresa nacional. *EAD em Foco: Revista Científica em Educação a Distância, 1*(1), 145-158.

Filatro, A. (2004). *Design instrucional contextualizado [Contextual instructional design].* São Paulo: Editora Senac.

Tessmer, M., & Richey, R. C. (1997). The role of context in learning and instructional design. *Educational Technology Research and Development, 45*(2), 85-115.

Vygotsky, L. (1987). *A formação social da mente: o desenvolvimento dos processos psicológicos superiores [Mind in society: The development of higher psychological processes].* São Paulo: Martins Fontes.

8. Readiness for Inter-Institutional Collaboration: A Path Forward For Online Learning

Robert A. Paulson. Chair of Exercise Science. Pacific Union College, Angwin, United States. Corresponding Author: bpaulson@puc.edu

Shirley Freed. Chair, School of Education. Burman University, Lacombe, Canada

Abstract

An environment conducive to inter-institutional collaboration greater utilizes intellectual and structural assets for the good of all in a growing learning community. As small colleges and universities struggle to maintain financial viability many have recognized the positive impact a collaborative environment has for all aspects of the institution. The leaders in this transition from autonomous to collaborative have been librarians in their use of technology to share databases and other assets. Organizations like the Concordia University System and The Great Plains Interactive Distance Education Alliance have been sharing structural and intellectual assets to reduce costs and risks in offering online learning. Shared assets can be as simple as professors or classes from another institution, webinars for discussing online pedagogy, or as complicated as a shared Student Information System. The dropping of the traditional institutional boundary to form a closer and more collaborative relationship has a history of challenges. Conversely, as financial constraints increase, the need to overcome those previously overwhelming challenges has inspired creativity and the accomplishment of what was previously thought to be impossible. This study used the Transtheoretical Model of Behavioral Change to assess the current status of inter-institutional collaboration among 15 Adventist colleges and universities in North America. The data gave evidence that the majority of faculty were at the precontemplation stage while the majority of administrators were at the maintenance stage. The intermediate/outcome measures of decisional balance, self-efficacy, and behavioral frequency had a significant relationship with the stage of inter-institutional collaboration. This kind of stage-associated behavior supports the Transtheoretical Model.

The Purpose of the Study

The marketplace challenges of limited endowments and fluctuating enrollments have caused many smaller institutions to respond to the challenge by forming consortiums such as Claremont Colleges, Five Colleges Inc., Concordia University System, and The Great Plains Interactive Distance Education Alliance. (Diessner, 1998; Edington, 2006; Sanders, 2011). By working together these small institutions accomplish what they would not have been able to do alone. They share intellectual and structural assets such as servers, student information systems, learning management systems, program curricula, and, where geographical location permits, Student Life programming. These kinds of alliances have been found to lower costs and the risks related to the implementation of new programs (Dabl, 2003).

Seventh-day Adventist higher education institutions in North America face the environmental challenges of an aging church membership, declining economic status among members, and membership growth in ethnic populations that traditionally do not participate in higher education (Osborn, 2007; Van Der Werf, 1999; Widmer, 1994).

The purpose of this study was to describe the current status of inter-institutional collaboration among Adventist institutions of higher education in North America. Without a clear understanding of the status of inter-institutional collaboration and the demographic issues involved, the outlook for moving the organization forward to a more inter-institutionally collaborative environment is bleak (J. O. Prochaska, Velicer, DiClemente, & Fava, 1988; Levesque, Prochaska, & Prochaska, 2001).

For the purpose of this study, the definition of inter-institutional collaboration was set at a conservative level in hopes of documenting any collaborative initiatives, small or large, within NAD Adventist higher education. In the book *Organizing Higher Education for Collaboration* (2009), Kezar and Lester make the following statement: "To make collaboration successful, organizations need to be redesigned to enhance group and cross-divisional work, which otherwise typically fails" (p. 36). The definition used in this study asks little in the way of a redesign for Adventist higher education but does require open lines of communication, respect, and a willingness to trust colleagues from other institutions. Central to the definition is an understanding that there are areas of commonality in mission and philosophical underpinnings that drive individuals and institutions.

Specifically, successful Inter-Institutional Collaboration requires that Faculty/Administrators:

1. Work with faculty/administrators from other NAD institutions of higher education by providing funding and or planning opportunities for inter-institutional academic/administrative programs/institutes;
2. Are involved in inter-institutional purchasing or financial projects/ventures with the goal of minimizing costs and maximizing financial resources;
3. Share professional resources such as teaching or administrative documents and procedures;
4. Participate at least once a term in brainstorming sessions with colleagues of like job assignments on topics such as scholarly exchange and discussion of pedagogical or administrative issues.

Theoretical Framework

The Transtheoretical Model (TTM) of human behavioral change was used to evaluate the status of inter-institutional collaboration among Adventist institutions of higher education in North America. This model was developed by James O. Prochaska and has been used to assess a variety of behavioral changes, such as smoker to non-smoker, within health-related fields (J. M. Prochaska et al., 2005; J. O. Prochaska et al., 1988; J. O. Prochaska, Norcross, & DiClemente, 1994; J. O. Prochaska & Norcross, 2001) and to describe organizational change (Levesque et al., 2001). The model has two parts: the stages of change and the processes by which change occurs. The stages are precontemplation (not thinking about changing the behavior), contemplation (thinking about changing the behavior), preparation (looking for ways to change the behavior), action (working to change the behavior), and maintenance (the behavior has been changed and the person or organization is working to maintain the change) (J. O. Prochaska, Velicer, et al., 1994).

As part of the stage-of-change assessment, the Transtheoretical Model includes intermediate outcome measures that are stage-associated and enhance the power of the TTM to accurately assess the person or organization's stage of change. These measures are decisional balance (pro and con), self-efficacy, and behavioral frequency. As the person or organization moves from precontemplation to maintenance, the participant sees the change of behavior as increasingly positive or pro, or decreasingly negative or con. The participant's confidence in his or her ability to make the change increases along with the frequency of participation in the desired behavior.

Once the status or stage of change has been evaluated, the Transtheoretical Model suggests activities or processes that increase the likelihood of inspiring change. These processes or activities are either covert or overt activities engaged in by people or organizations to alter emotions, thinking, behaviors, or relationships (J. O. Prochaska & DiClemente, 1984; Levesque et al., 2001). There are 10 processes used to help move people along the stages of change. The first five are experiential in nature and are most productive during the stages of precontemplation, contemplation, and preparation. The experiential processes are consciousness raising, dramatic relief, environmental re-evaluation, social liberation, and self-re-evaluation. The second five are behavioral in nature and are best suited for participants in the stages of action and maintenance. The behavioral processes are stimulus control, helping relationships, counter conditioning, reinforcement management, and self-liberation (J. O. Prochaska, Norcross, et al., 1994; J. O. Prochaska & Norcross, 2003).

Research Design

This study was quantitative in design using survey research methodology developed by James O. Prochaska, J. C. Norcross, & C. C. DiClemente (1994) and was adapted to assess inter-institutional collaboration among Adventist institutions of higher education in North America. The survey was administered via web-based technology (Zoomerang) to faculty and administrators at 15 of the 15 Adventist institutions of higher education in North America. The survey attempted to collect data from the entire population of faculty and administrators working at Adventist institutions of higher education in North America. The rationale for inclusion of the entire population was twofold. First, the return rate on web-based surveys is traditionally low (Andrews, D., Nonnecke, B., & Preece, J. 2003) and by sampling the entire population, data were gathered from a larger percentage of the total population. The actual return rate for this study was 32% or 797 out of the total population of 2,578. Andrews et al. (2003) found that response rates of as low as 20% would not be considered uncommon for this type of survey. Secondarily, web-based surveys make it possible to survey the entire population at no additional expense.

Results

The study population had representation from 15 of the 15 Adventist institutions of higher education. Of the participants who responded to demographic questions, there were 301 females and 330 males, 494 faculty, and 137 administrators. Thirty-eight percent of the administrators and 22% of the faculty working at Adventist institutions of higher education in North America participated in the study.

The participants had a mean age of 52.5 years, with the faculty at 52.1 and the administrators at 54.0 years of age. The mean for years of experience in Adventist higher education was 15.5 years, with administrators at 17.7 years and faculty at 14.9. Of the 631 participants, 389 (60.5%) have had experience outside Adventist higher education. Of the participants with experience outside of Adventist higher education, 273 (42.5%) participants had experience in non-Adventist higher education, 122 (19.0%) in secondary education, and 78 (12.1%) at the kindergarten to eighth-grade level. The survey listed 20 possible teaching assignments for faculty, with nursing as the most often selected at 14% of the participating faculty. Of the possible 15 presidents, 4 participated, with vice-presidents for student services as the most participatory group of vice-presidents.

Research Question 1

What is the status of inter-institutional collaboration among Adventist colleges and universities in North America?

As a population, the majority of the participants are either in pre-contemplation and contemplation (57%) or action and maintenance (42%) (Figure 8.1). For further analysis, the 1% of participants in the preparation stage was combined with the participants in contemplation. Note that the majority of participants are either in the precontemplation or maintenance stage. Very few are in the process of making a decision to participate in inter-institutional collaboration; likewise, there are very few in the early stages of taking action.

Figure 8.1 Participants' stage frequency distribution in percentage of total.

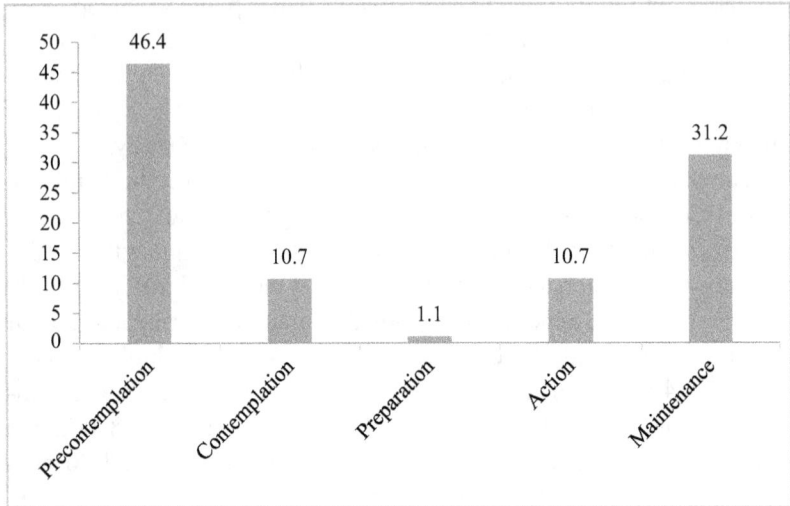

Research Question 2

What is the relationship between the stages of inter-institutional collaboration and the following selected demographic character-istics: gender, work classification, age, and years of experience in Adventist higher education?

A Chi-Square analysis indicated that stage of collaboration is not related to gender (χ^2 =1.75, df=3, p=0.627), whereas work classifica-tion as faculty or administration (χ^2 =33.52, df=3, p=0.000), age of the participant (χ^2 =23.33, df=9, p=0.005), and years of experience in Adventist higher education (χ^2 =18.21, df=6, p=0.006) do have a sig-nificant relationship with stage of inter-institutional collaboration. The majority of faculty (52%) are at the precontemplative stage whereas the majority of administrators are at the maintenance stage (49%).The data also indicate that even though the majority of a work classifica-tion group may be at one extreme, there is still a considerable number of that group at the other end of the stages of change (Figure 2).

Further investigation into the significance of the relationship of age and stage demonstrated that when faculty (χ^2 =16.57, df=9, p=0.056), and administrators (χ^2 =15.04, df=9, p=0.090) were analyzed sepa-rately, there was no significant relationship between age and stage of inter-institutional collaboration.

Further analysis of the relationship of the years of experience and stage of inter-institutional collaboration revealed that when work assignment groups were analyzed separately, only faculty demonstrated a significant relationship between years of experience and stage of collaboration ($\chi^2 =8.77$, $df=3$, $p=0.033$). Those with fewer years of experience are less likely to be at the maintenance stage of inter-institutional collaboration.

Figure 8.2 Participants' stage frequency distribution percentages within work classification.

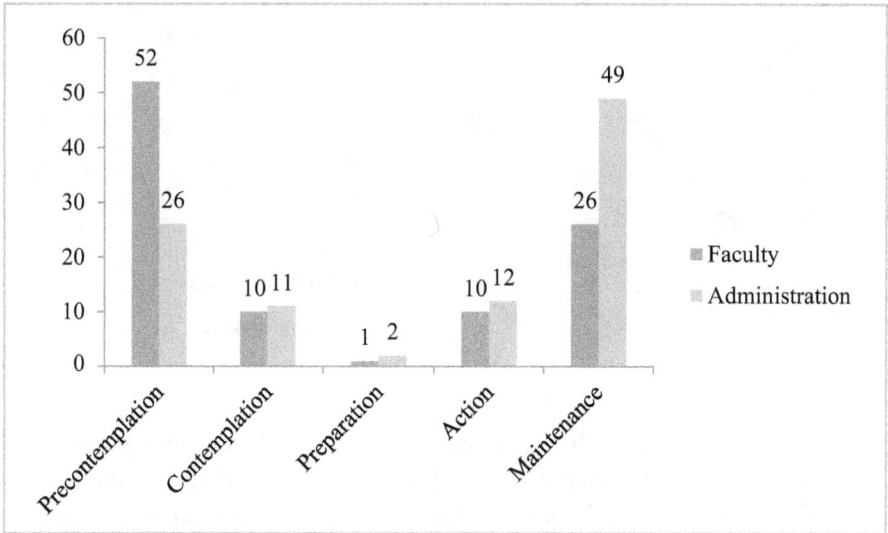

Research Question 3

What is the relationship between stage of inter-institutional collaboration and scores on decisional balance, self-efficacy, and behavioral frequency?

A significant ($\alpha \leq .01$) relationship was found between stage of inter-institutional collaboration and participants' scores on decisional balance (pro, $p=.000$; con, $p=.010$); self-efficacy ($p=.000$), and behavioral frequency ($p=.000$). A graphic representation of the stage-associated changes in decisional balance can be seen in Figure 8.3.

Figure 8.3 Stage-associated changes in decisional balance.

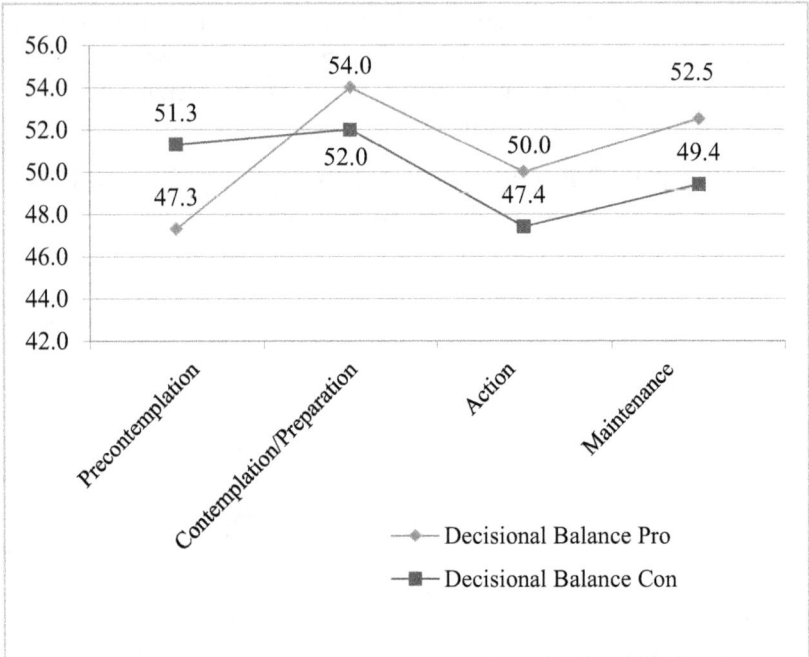

Post hoc analysis identified areas of significant change in pro scores to be between precontemplation and contemplation/preparation ($p=.000$) and again from precontemplation to maintenance ($p=.000$). The con scores demonstrated a significant stage-associated difference between the stages of precontemplation and action ($p=.021$) and between contemplation/preparation and action ($p=.046$).

Participants' self-efficacy scores at precontemplation had a mean value of 2.15 and 2.56 at maintenance. The post-hoc analysis identified participants' self-efficacy scores at precontemplation to be significantly different from scores at maintenance ($p=.000$). A graphic representation of this stage-associated change in self-efficacy can be seen in Figure 8.4. This kind of increase in participants' self-efficacy, related to behavioral change, is in line with the Transtheoretical Model and gives evidence of its use in the organizational setting.

Figure 8.4 Stage-associated changes in self-efficacy.

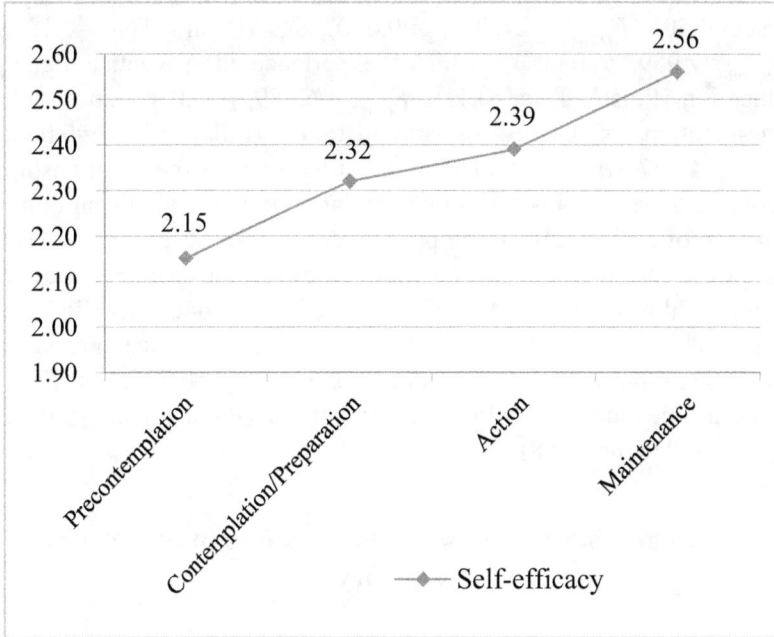

Participant stage-associated scores for behavioral frequency were found to be significantly different in all stage combinations. A graphic presentation of the progression of behavioral frequency from precontemplation to maintenance can be seen in Figure 8.5. The survey questions related to behavioral frequency are target-behavior-associated and support the definition of inter-institutional collaboration used in this study. The fact that the data in this study demonstrated significant stage-associated changes in behavioral frequency supports the theory of intermediate outcome measures within the Transtheoretical Model.

Research Question 4

In the context of gender, age, years of experience in Adventist higher education, and classification as faculty or administrator, what is the relationship between the stage of inter-institutional collaboration and scores of decisional balance, self-efficacy, and behavioral frequency?

There is a significant relationship between stage of inter-institutional collaboration and the linear combination of decisional balance pro and con, self-efficacy, and behavioral frequency. However, there is no significant interaction effect between stage of inter-institutional collaboration and the demographic characteristics of gender (Pillai's Trace=0.505, $F_{(12,1644)}$=27.701, p=0.000), age (Pillai's Trace=0.129, $F_{(9,1596)}$=7.959, p=0.000), years of experience in Adventist higher education (Pillai's Trace=0.116, $F_{(9,1503)}$=6.689, p=0.000), and work classification as faculty or administrator (Pillai's Trace=0.066, $F_{(9,1707)}$=4.237, p=0.000). The data suggest that the relationship between stage of inter-institutional collaboration and the linear combination of decisional balance pro and con, self-efficacy, and behavioral frequency does not depend on the demographic characteristics of gender (Pillai's Trace=0.018, $F_{(12,1644)}$=0.805, p=0.646), age (Pillai's Trace=0.032, $F_{(9,1569)}$=0.646, p=0.919), years of experience in Adventist higher education (Pillai's Trace=0.026, $F_{(18,1503)}$=0.737, p=0.775), and classification as faculty or administrator (Pillai's Trace=0.015, $F_{(9,1707)}$=0.976, p=0.458).

Figure 8.5 Stage-associated changes in behavioral frequency.

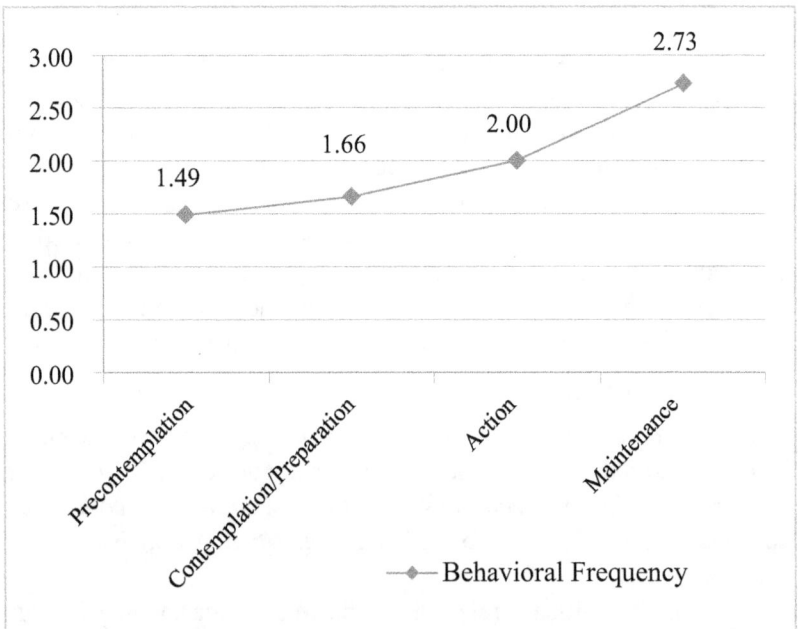

Scholarly Significance

In this section, we offer some possible explanations for the results as well as provide suggestions for stage matching. A review of current faculty initiatives and organizations demonstrates that within Adventist higher education, small informal, and, to a limited extent, formal networks of faculty have been created. These small networks have crossed institutional boundaries and connected like-minded individuals, opened avenues of trust, and broadened the members' understanding of Adventist higher education and the need for inter-institutional collaboration. Casual networking has been made possible by subject-area national meetings, the job-related transition of faculty members to other Adventist institution of higher education, or by the close-knit connections that exist within the Adventist church in North America. One such casual network that became formal was the creation of the Adventist Virtual Learning Lab (AVLL) or, as it was later known, Adventist Virtual Learning Network (AVLN). In 1999, a group of faculty recognized the need for collaboration in distributed or online learning and organized a conference in Orlando, Florida. The conference involved discussions related to collaboration in online learning but was driven on the collective understanding that "together we stand, divided we fall" (Eggers, 2001). On a more formal basis, faculty are involved in academic organizations, which have been established by departments or academic disciplines such as English, Physical Education, and Religion. These organizations meet in conjunction with national conventions but attendance is limited due to budgetary constraints.

In contrast to the faculty, administrators describe themselves as predominately in the maintenance stage (48.6%) of inter-institutional collaboration with a significant portion (26.1%) in precontemplation. The degree of availability and the extent of networking opportunities for collaboration inherent in the job of an administrator may be a contributory factor. Administrators at Adventist institutions of higher education in North America are members of a variety of committees or organizations functioning at the North American Division level. Those committees or organizations include the Association of Adventist Colleges and Universities (AACU), the Adventist Distance Education Consortium (ADEC), Adventist Student Personnel Association (ASSPA), and the North American Division Association of College and University Business Officers (NAD-ACUBO). These organizations meet on a regular basis and stay in touch with their members via newsletters and email distribution lists. This kind of networking enhances the opportunity for collaboration and opens the doors of communication between colleagues across institutional boundaries. However, the question must be asked, why are a significant number of administrators in the precontemplative stage (26.3%)?

With the availability of networking opportunities and job descriptions that demand a clear understanding of institutional challenges, why do some administrators seem to fail to consider inter-institutional collaboration as holding potential for enhancing institutional viability? One might suggest that as institutions are faced with greater financial challenges, administrators become consumed in the process of maintaining their own institution and lose sight of the prospect of a systems approach to meeting institutional challenges. As a previous member of the Adventist Digital Education Consortium (ADEC) (now disbanded), we have observed this kind of institutional focus in action. One of the projects undertaken by ADEC was a cross-registration program for online classes. This program would have made online classes offered at Adventist institutions of higher education in North America available, within block tuition plans, to students attending other Adventist institutions of higher education in North America. After many attempts, the cross-registration program failed to reach implementation due to individual institutional financial concerns. The inability to enact this type of inter-institutionally collaborative program demonstrates behavior congruent with a population at the precontemplative stage of inter-institutional collaboration.

Review of the data from this study demonstrates that during the combined stages of contemplation/preparation the perception of the change to inter-institutional collaboration became increasingly positive and outweighed the negatives into the stages of action and maintenance. As long as people involved in the change process believe that the change process is inherently negative, they will resist making the desired change in behavior. Previous research has observed average increases in decisional balance pro scores of 1.0 standard deviations and decreases in con scores of 0.5 standard deviations in the transition between precontemplation and action (Prochaska, Norcross et al., 1994). The previous research involved a variety of populations and behaviors and does not suggest that the degree of change in stage-associated decisional balance scores observed in this study is out of the norm. What is of particular interest is the drop in pro scores as the participant moves from contemplation/preparation to action (Figure 3). The decline in participants' positive attitude relative to a change in behavior may be caused as the person initiates implementation of inter-institutional collaborative activities and encounters unantici-pated challenges. In other words, as people in an organization move from the decision-making stage to the implementation or action, their initial feelings of optimism, relative to the change in behavior, are diminished by the reality making the change. For example, the cross-registration program for students in Adventist higher education would have made available online classes taught at AACU member schools available, free of charge, to students at students attending other AACU member institutions. However, cross-registration has failed implementation caused by a variety of economic and institu-tional challenges. It is this kind of organizational change challenge that could easily decrease attitudes relative to the positive nature of inter-institutional collaboration.

This study found that the intermediate/outcome measures of decisional balance, self-efficacy, and behavioral frequency had a significant relationship with the stage of inter-institutional collabora-tion within the total participant population and within demographic groups. This kind of stage-associated behavior supports the Trans-theoretical Model's hypothesis that as a person or organization moves from precontemplation to maintenance, there will be stage-associated changes in the intermediate/outcome measures, thus enhancing the model's ability to describe the behavioral change.

In light of the results of this study, we recommend a stage-matched approach focused on enhancing the environment for inter-institution-al collaboration among Adventist institutions of higher education in North America. However, without the support of individual institu-tions, conferences, divisions, and the General Conference of Seventh-day Adventists, attempts to enhance inter-institutional collaboration in Adventist higher education will likely fail.

Experiential Stage Matching

In general terms, participants in precontemplation and contempla-tion need the interventions that are experiential in nature and include the processes of consciousness raising, dramatic relief, environmental re-evaluation, social liberation, and self-re-evaluation. The following recommended interventions meet the change needs of participants in the stages of precontemplation and contemplation:

1. Communication with participants in regard to the value of and goals for inter-institutional collaboration in Adventist higher education,
2. Opportunities to inspire interest in inter-institutional collaboration and alleviate participants' anxiety associated with the change,
3. Communication that increases understanding of the interconnected nature of Adventist higher education and how individual institutions can benefit from increased inter-institutional collaboration,
4. A concerted effort on the part of leadership to express commitment to inter-institutional collaboration. Expressions of commitment need to be clear and financially supported at all levels of administration from the individual institutions to the General Conference of Seventh-day Adventists.

Behavioral Stage Matching

In general terms, participants in action and maintenance need interventions that are more behavioral in nature and include the processes of stimulus control, helping relationships, counter conditioning, reinforcement management, and self-liberation. The following recommended interventions meet the change needs of participants in the stages of action and maintenance:

1. The creation of a structure that produces incentives to maintain or advance stages of inter-institutional collaboration.
2. Provide financial support for individuals and institutions desiring to explore greater involvement in inter-institutional collaboration.
3. Develop and publicize a strategic plan for inter-institutional collaboration among Adventist institutions of higher education in North America.

Other Strategic Initiatives

The following recommended strategic initiatives offer environments that are both experiential and behavioral in nature. Special attention should be given to guiding participants into aspects of the activities that meet stage-related needs.

1. Support the creation of a higher education convention, which would include all faculty and administrators working at Adventist institutions of higher education in North America. The convention would offer participants an opportunity to network with colleagues from other institutions, share experiences in the field of inter-institutional collaboration, and explore the possibilities of involvement in inter-institutional collaboration initiatives. At the same time, participants at the stages of action and maintenance could be given recognition for their participation in inter-institutional collaboration and support for further exploration within the concept of collaboration.

2. Financially support the creation and utilization of a variety of asynchronous communities focused on areas of interest to faculty and administrators and matched to the participants' stage of inter-institutional collaboration. Communication in these communities would be via discussion forums, distribution lists, podcasts, and newsletters. Geographic and time issues are a challenge to the process of networking colleagues in Adventist higher education, thus the use of asynchronous communication would reduce those challenges and enhance networking opportunities.

3. Financially support an increase in the frequency and quality of regular synchronous communication between colleagues of similar academic, social, and work interest via face-to-face meetings, video conferencing, and webinars. This type of interaction would be of great value to participants in the early stages of inter-institutional collaboration such as young faculty needing to establish collaborative networks.

4. Create and encourage the use of a learning object repository where intellectual assets could be shared and improved upon. Assets shared in this repository would be part of an environment for collaboration where participants would benefit from the work of others. In order to ensure success, steps need to be taken to publicize the creation of the repository and reward its use.

5. Support the creation of a Council for Collaboration in Adventist Higher Education, which would include leadership representation by faculty and administrators at the institutional, Union, North American Division, and General Conference

levels. This council would be given authority to reward and provide incentives to promote inter-institutionally collaborative efforts by institutions and individuals.

6. Give faculty and administrators working at institutions of higher education in North America opportunities to take classes from other Adventist institutions of higher education in North America at no charge.

Conclusion

Continued research into the status of inter-institutional collaboration and the effectiveness of the processes of change used by Seventh-day Adventist higher education to enhance inter-institutional collaboration would add to the body of knowledge relative to organizational change and the effectiveness of the Transtheoretical Model in the organizational environment. As Adventist higher education in North America continues to work to meet the needs of the learner and overcome the challenges of the changing financial and sociological environment of higher education, it must continually evaluate the effectiveness of its efforts and work to gain a better understanding of its inter-institutional collaborative status.

Kezar and Lester (2009) make the following statement: "To make collaboration successful, organizations need to be redesigned to enhance group and cross-divisional work, which otherwise typically fails" (p. 36). Adventist higher education is in the beginning stages of transforming into a more collaborative environment and thus needs to re-evaluate its structure, with the goal of increased inter-institutional collaboration.

If Adventist higher education is going to meet the challenge of creating a holistic educational experience within the current economic and sociological environment, the 15 Adventist institutions of higher education in North America need to work together in a spirit of collaboration for the good of all, especially the students.

Robert A. Paulson

Robert is a Professor and the Chair of the Exercise Science department at Pacific Union College. He is also an Adjunct Professor at Eastern Oregon University and has done adjunct work for Walla Walla University and Andrews University. He enjoys a wide variety of teaching modalities and strives to be creative no matter the type or location of his classroom. Bob's most notable online endeavors are an online Jogging class taught for Eastern Oregon University and his service as President of Adventist Virtual Learning Network from 2007 to 2016.

Shirley Freed

Shirley has been actively involved in online education for about 20 years as an online teacher, administrator, and researcher. She has facilitated the development of online courses and programs and has received awards for her exemplary courses. Although she is currently spending most of her time in administration, she will always be a teacher first, whether online or face-to-face. Shirley also served as President of Adventist Virtual Learning Network from 1999 to 2006.

References

Andrews, D., Nonnecke, B., & Preece, J. (2003). Electronic survey methodology: A case study in researching hard to involve Internet users. *International Journal of Human Computer Interaction, 16*, 185-210.

Dabl, J. (2003). Inter-institutional alliances lower costs and risks. *Distance Education Report, 9*, 3-6.

Diessner, J. (1998). Beyond flubber: Technology makes interinstitutional collaboration a reality. *About Campus. 3*, 23.

Edington, P. R. (2006). Chief academic officers in New England community colleges: leadership and regional collaboration. *Dissertation Abstracts International, 67*, 04A.

Eggers, M. (2001). Adventist virtual learning laboratory. *Journal of Adventist Education, 63*, 39-42.

Kezar, A. J., & Lester, J. (2009). *Organizing higher education for collaboration.* San Francisco, CA: Jossey-Bass.

Levesque, D. A., Prochaska, J. M., & Prochaska, J. O. (1999). Stages of change and integrated service delivery. *Consulting Psychology Journal, 51*, 226-241.

Levesque, D. A., Prochaska, J. M., & Prochaska, J. O., Dewart, S. R., Hamby, L. S., & Weeks, W. P. (2001). Organizational stages and processes of change for continuous quality improvement in health care. *Consulting Psychology Journal, 53*, 139-153.

Osborn, R. (2007, February). *Facing our challenges.* Paper presented at the meeting of the Association of Adventist Colleges and Universities Higher Education Conference on Mission, Orlando, FL.

Prochaska, J. M., Paiva, A. L., Padula, J. A., Prochaska, J. O., Montgomery, J. E., Hageman, L., & Bergart, A. M. (2005). Assessing emotional readiness for adoption using the Transtheoretical Model. *Children and Youth Services Review, 27,* 135-153.

Prochaska, J. O. & DiClemente, C.C. (1984). The transtheoretical approach: Crossing the traditional boundaries of therapy. Melbourne, Florida: Krieger Publishing Company

Prochaska, J. O., & Norcross, J. C. (2001). Stages of change. *Psychotherapy: Theory, Research, Practice, Training, 38*, 443-448.

Prochaska, J. O., & Norcross, J. C. (2003). *Systems of psychotherapy: A transtheoretical analysis.* Pacific Grove, CA: Thomson.

Prochaska, J. O., Norcross, J. C., & DiClemente, C. C. (1994). Changing for good: A revolutionary six-stage program for overcoming bad habits and moving your life positively forward. New York, NY: HarperCollins.

Prochaska, J. O., Velicer, W. F., DiClemente, C. C., & Fava, J. (1988). Measuring processes of change: Applications to the cessation of smoking. *Journal of Consulting and Clinical Psychology, 56,* 520-528.

Prochaska, J. O., Velicer, W. F., Rossi, J. S., Goldstein, M. G., Marcus, B. H., Rakowski, W., . . . Rossi, S.R. (1994). Stages of change and decisional balance for 12 problem behaviors. *Health Psychology, 13,* 39-46.

Sanders, G. (2011). The Great Plains IDEA gerontology program: An online interinstitutional graduate degree. *Gerontology & Geriatrics Education, 23,* 233-244.

Van Der Werf, M. (1999). The precarious balancing act at small liberal-arts colleges. *Chronicle of Higher Education, 45,* 32-35.

Widmer, M. (1994). Brainstorming the future for Adventist colleges and universities. *Adventist Review, 171,* 15-17.

Effectiveness

Online education is continually in a pursuit of quality and effectiveness. Many factors impact student perception of the efficacy of online learning. In this section, the chapters explore a variety of components of effectiveness, including the learning management system experience, the teaching and learning experience, and the course design. David Jeffrey and Randy Siebold explore faculty perceptions and the use of the learning management system (LMS) and their relationship to successful implementation of the LMS. Nancy Liliana Herrera Villamizar, Dora Patricia Martínez Cebreros, and Caterina Evelin Pavoni share the results of their research on the impact of teaching and instructional design on student satisfaction and retention. Prema Gaikwad and Mak Chung Yin present the results of studying student perceptions of the effectiveness of online learning, concluding that four aspects are key for success: (a) student autonomy, (b) instructional design, (c) interactivity, and (d) learning environment and resources.

9. Upgrading Learning Management Systems: Understanding Faculty Perceptions and Use for Improved Implementation

David A. Jeffrey. Assistant Professor, Business. Burman University, Lacombe, Canada. Corresponding Author: david.jeffrey@gmail.com

Randy J. Siebold. Associate Professor, Leadership. Andrews University, Berrien Springs, United States

Abstract

Like most colleges and universities, Adventist schools are in a constantly changing academic environment and are under consistent pressure to implement the latest technologies, such as Learning Management Systems (LMSs). This research study seeks to provide a better understanding of faculty perceptions of their LMS by using a survey developed from the Technology Acceptance Model 3 with the addition of change fatigue. The results helped us determine what factors lead to successful use of LMSs by faculty. Responses to two hundred surveys from nine North American Adventist universities explored the factors that lead to intention and use. The study highlighted seven important factors in the implementation of an LMS. These factors included: Perceptions of LMSs, Experience, User Participation, Training, Peer Support, Voluntariness, and Change Fatigue. We expect that those administrating and directing Learning Management Systems that consider these factors will be more likely to experience successful implementation.

Introduction

The category of software programs known as Learning Management Systems (LMS) has arisen in response to the educational desire to organize and administer instruction with Internet-hosted learning materials (Gautreau, 2011, p. 13). An LMS is defined as "software that has been used in a learning content presentation which has a significant role and complexity in [an] e-learning environment" (Aydin

& Tirkes, 2010, p. 176). An LMS "provides a place for learning and teaching activities to occur within a seamless environment" (Unal & Unal, 2011, p. 19). In short, while there is still discussion regarding a precise definition of many of these terms (Moore, Dickson-Deane, & Gaylen, 2011; Watson & Watson, 2007), we refer to an LMS as an interactive website that enables faculty to both provide learning materials and track participation and progress of students. The LMS industry, like most technology-based industries, is in a continual state of transition as it has been since it began (Beatty & Ulasewicz, 2006). As a result, universities must constantly review, update, and upgrade their software to provide faculty and students with online learning tools that are reliable, simple, powerful, and intuitive.

Faculty members determine, to a large degree, the rate of adoption they pursue. When describing those resistant to adoption, Talke and Heidenreich (2014) suggest that they can have a predisposition to resist change rather than naturally accepting it. This challenging response is even more likely when faculty have seen many changes in their careers—some have been helpful, but often the changes are short-lived and seen largely as a waste of time. The faculty can experience change fatigue—"a sense of malaise, frustration, and cynicism that any change effort was destined to fail" (Ace & Parker, 2010, p. 21). Understandably, administrators and those tasked with directing LMSs are deeply interested in making decisions that will lead to a quick and low-hassle adoption of technology within their educational systems.

Adventist higher education is no exception. We expect that the faculty in these institutions hold perspectives towards technology changes, some positive and others negative. We also expect that many within these institutions seek to better understand their faculty's perceptions.

Fortunately, the TAM 3 (Technology Acceptance Model 3) can help us better understand what faculty intend to do (Behavioral Intention) and their resulting implementation (Use Behavior) (Venkatesh & Bala, 2008). The TAM 3 model also focuses on the determinants that influence how faculty perceive the usefulness of the technology (Perceived Usefulness) and how easy the innovation is to use (Perceived Ease of Use).

Using the TAM 3 as a theoretical framework, this study seeks to better understand the factors that influence the use behavior of LMSs by faculty members among nine Adventist institutions of higher learning in North America. In addition, this study evaluates how change fatigue impacts the adoption process.

Relevant Literature

Much study has been undertaken regarding innovation and specifically how technological innovation impacts organizations. Everett Rogers (2003) is perhaps the grandfather of innovation, through his book *Diffusion of Innovation*, now in its fifth edition. Rogers identified five groups of people whose behaviors enable innovations to move from being considered risky to being well accepted: innovators, early adopters, early majority, late majority, and laggards. Understanding and using Rogers' principles can assist administrators in understanding their faculty and helping them to move toward adoption.

Moreover, barriers also exist to hamper the adoption of new technologies, particularly in higher education. Introducing adaptive learning technologies, such as LMSs, comes with the expectation that more students will be educated at a lower cost with at least similar, but hopefully better educational outcomes (Bacow, Bowen, Guthrie, Long, & Lack, 2012). In evaluating the structures in educational institutions, it is important to notice that some structures may be both barriers to and drivers for change. As such, careful analysis is required to know how to manage structures (Svanström, et al., 2012).

Carter (2008) looked at the model Kurt Lewin (1947) originated, in which the organization needs first to unfreeze its members by convincing them of the need for change. After the change, refreezing is necessary to ensure that the organization's new course is reinforced by its procedures and practices.

Carter also indicated that an important part of successful change is that the skills transfer to those affected by the change. The development of skills ensures that acceptance of the change comes more easily. Carter also created a seven-step model: "set up for success, create urgency, shape the future, implement, support the shift, sustain momentum, and stabilize the environment" (Carter, 2008, p. 23).

Organizational learning is critical for success in higher education organizational change. The kinds of change involved with the change of an operating system is a transformational kind of change, requiring that the innovation be brought into the institution's boundaries and aligned with its culture in order to be successful (Boyce, 2003).

Tools such as inquiry, dialogue, and action learning can be helpful in creating a culture of learning within an organization that will facilitate change.

Understanding barriers to change is important because the fear, panic, and skepticism they may create can lead to resistance, disengagement, and burnout (Auster & Ruebottom, 2013). Many barriers are related to the response of faculty to the technology. Some faculty appreciate the relationships they have with students and feel that technologies will disrupt that relationship, creating distance between them and their students (Bacow, et al., 2012; Francis & Shannon, 2013). Another concern is that the technology will reduce their job security, as the online systems are perceived to replace faculty jobs (Bacow, et al., 2012; Francis & Shannon, 2013; Shannon, Francis, & Torpey, 2012).

An integrative model of the factors limiting the adoption of innovation (Schiavone & MacVaugh, 2009) looked at several factors that influence when new technology will not replace older technology. As far as technology is concerned, certain conditions seem to predict when new technologies will fail to replace their older counterpart: when users perceive the utility of the innovation to be less than the older technology; when the innovation is so complex that it causes users to focus more on the overall effectiveness rather than on the newest features; and when using older technologies with other items leads to higher total utility than when using newer technologies. Specifically in the domain of learning, when the capacity to learn is limited or the access to education is limited, when what the users learned to use the older product doesn't help them with the innovation, and when the switching costs are high, newer technology runs a high risk of not replacing the older technology.

In the realm of higher education, technological change is influenced by professors' perceptions of risk. The greater the feeling of risk that a new technology will bring, the greater can be the reluctance of teachers to embrace the new technology. Howard (2011) discovered that the willingness of teachers to accept risk is linked to teachers' affect for technology and the value of the technology in teaching. The appreciation and openness of teachers, and the positive feelings that they have toward technology, combined with the positive impact the technology can have on the educational experience, appear to increase the willingness of teachers to innovate with technology.

Methodology

This research study was an empirical, non-experimental, descriptive, and confirmatory quantitative study, using survey methods that were built on the TAM 3 within the context of a sample of North American Adventist university faculty. This design allowed one-time data collection, and enabled several comparisons of relevant variables across different universities, different learning management systems, genders, age groups, etc. Path analysis was conducted in instances where there was a possible mediated influence of one or more variables.

The subjects for the study were faculty members from nine Adventist institutions of higher learning, including Andrews University, Burman University, La Sierra University, Loma Linda University, Pacific Union College, Southern Adventist University, Southwestern Adventist University, Union College, and Washington Adventist University. The population of the study was limited to full-time salaried faculty members who use LMSs.

Since the calculated number of faculty members at the nine institutions was 2000, the target sample size was set at 10% of the total full-time faculty members at the nine institutions, 200. This number of participants yielded a margin of error of approximately 6.56%. With 203 completed surveys, and three dropped because of abnormalities, the final N was 200 respondents.

Results and Discussion

The results are reported for the following factors: Perceptions of LMSs, Experience, User Participation, Training, Peer Support, Voluntariness, and Change Fatigue.

Perceptions of Learning Management Systems

The four LMSs in use at the studied universities were *Blackboard*, *Canvas*, *Desire2Learn* (now branded as *BrightSpace*), and *Moodle*. Post hoc comparisons using the Bonferroni method with an alpha of .05 found that for faculty Use Behavior, *Canvas* ($M = 5.07$) was used significantly more than *Moodle* ($M = 3.98$), *D2L* ($M = 3.63$), and *Blackboard* ($M = 3.31$). For Perceived Usefulness, *Canvas* ($M = 6.26$) was found to be significantly more useful than *Moodle* ($M = 5.14$), *Blackboard* ($M = 4.63$), and *D2L* ($M = 4.50$). For Perceived Ease of Use, *Canvas* ($M = 5.70$) was found to be significantly easier to use than *Blackboard* ($M = 4.33$), *Moodle* ($M = 4.27$), and *D2L* ($M = 3.96$).

The LMS *Canvas* achieves significantly higher ratings than all other LMSs on the three central variables with significant differences (Use Behavior, Perceived Usefulness, and Perceived Ease of Use). It is likely, however, that other factors, including Voluntariness, balance the values for Behavioral Intention. Behavioral Intention is not considered here because intent to use an LMS is more likely associated with administrative decision-making than with the faculty comparison of relative merit of a particular system. In fact, most faculty members would not be aware of the relative merits of the LMS used at their university as compared with others. The features of a specific LMS are more directly tied to faculty Perceived Usefulness and Perceived Ease of Use rather than a direct comparison to another system.

Additionally, while Use Behavior was demonstrated to be higher among *Canvas* users, there are likely to be additional factors involved in use, such as the requirement or campus culture towards the use of LMSs on the campuses where *Canvas* was used. We made no attempt to compare these variables in this study.

Experience

Not surprisingly, the data also reveal that faculty members with more experience (greater number of years teaching) were found to have lower scores in factors for successful LMS adoption. The following factors were each found to be statistically significant. Those faculty members with more experience: use the LMS less ($r=-.245$, $p<.001$), have lower intention to use it ($r=-.176$, $p=.006$), perceive the LMS as less useful ($r=-.194$, $p=.003$), perceive the LMS as more complex ($r=-.098$, $p=.083$ – marginally significant), perceive the LMS as less relevant to their job ($r=-.189$, $p=.004$), show lower computer playfulness ($r=-.154$, $p=.015$), have lower computer self-efficacy ($r=-.306$, $p<.001$), and demonstrate higher computer anxiety ($r=.168$, $p=.009$).

User Participation

User participation is primarily associated with the five predictors of Perceived Usefulness and Perceived Ease of Use. Faculty members, in cooperation with administrators who are involved in the process, will make efforts to maximize the benefit of these five predictor variables. Because of their efforts they will be keenly aware of why one system is chosen over another and why additional features are selected. This can then be communicated with enthusiasm to other faculty members. This communication will have far greater impact than a command decision and announcement from administration that "This is the system we have selected. Use it!"

Training

Training is a key intervention with any new innovation, and especially with technology-rich innovations. Training makes and reinforces connections between the technology and the duties of the faculty member, thus increasing Job Relevance. Training should occur several times, and as needed, to ensure that faculty with different levels of computer ability have enough opportunities to develop competence. Training clearly improves Output Quality and Result Demonstrability, as faculty members learn the features of the LMS. This enables faculty to get the most out of the LMS and trainers have the opportunity to make clear the benefits of the system so that faculty are able to explain them to others. In short, training is tied to enjoyment and perceived ease of use.

Peer Support

In addition to formal training, peer support interventions have been shown to influence Job Relevance, Output Quality, Result Demonstrability, and Perceptions of External Control. Others who have used and are familiar with LMSs can quickly share the qualities that make it relevant to the job, share tips for increasing the quality, and communicate the elements of the results that they have experienced, showing other faculty how to achieve similar results. Perceptions of External Control are enhanced as they feel in control of their LMS use through the support of their peers. Thus, peer support also encourages both Perceived Usefulness and Perceived Ease of Use.

Voluntariness

Another factor over which administration has direct control is Voluntariness. However, as dichotomous as the concept of "mandating usage" may be, as a variable it is surprisingly continuous. In fact, the actual distribution rates in the "excellent" range for skewness and kurtosis are normally distributed. This suggests that while administration at a particular university may mandate use of an LMS, faculty do not seem to view this as black and white. The variability of reaction is typically due to whether adherence or not has consequences.

For instance, one faculty member may say, "I have excellent resources that accomplish the same purpose as the LMS and would prefer to use them." If administration's response is "That seems fine," this encourages the perception that the requirement is not so absolute. On the other extreme, if administration docked pay for those who did not use the LMS, it is likely that everyone would use the LMS or change employment. However, history has demonstrated that an arbitrary unpopular decision may cause reactance (Brehm, 1966); that is, participants actually rebelling against use of the system.

An answer may seem to lie in an administrative decision that is supported by the faculty. For instance, if administration did an excellent job of selecting the best system, involving faculty in the process, demonstrating clear management support of the decision, organizing the LMS so that benefits were experienced by faculty, allowing faculty to have the best support, ensuring powerful organizational support, and creating structure for faculty to support one another, it is likely that an informed requirement might produce the best results.

Change Fatigue

While administration cannot directly influence Change Fatigue, decisions can be made that provide an environment that helps faculty deal with its effects. The goal is to facilitate faculty willingness to use an LMS despite the potential for frustration and cynicism that many changes can bring. However, the support from the leadership, organization, and peers all reduce frustration that may have been felt in the past with technology. Implementing effective training and clear alignment of incentives support will help encourage faculty.

Additionally, one must appreciate that change fatigue has typically developed over a number of years and reduction of change fatigue may be a long and gradual process. However, with consistent adherence by faculty and staff to wise selection choices, administrative and IT support, involvement of faculty in selection and modification of the LMS, and other recommended interventions, the incidence and severity of Change Fatigue can be reduced over time.

Application and Commentary

Faculty will use systems that are easy to use and that are relevant to their teaching practice. Some of the ease of use elements are predetermined by the selection of Learning Management System, as the study demonstrates significant differences in relevant factors among the various systems. *Canvas* is clearly the system that affords the greatest contributions toward faculty adoption and usage. For those unable or unwilling to change systems, other factors can be combined to increase the likelihood of adoption and use: effective training, mentorship from peer users, involvement of faculty in the system design and implementation processes, and careful attention to the amount and weight of change faced by faculty over time.

In this study, the faculty members from nine different Seventh-day Adventist universities were surveyed and the study highlighted eight important factors in the implementation of an LMS. These factors included: system relevance, output quality, result demonstrability, perceptions of external control, perceived enjoyment, voluntariness, and change fatigue. Faculty that perceive the system to be meaningful and useful in their daily work, and enjoyable to use, will use it. Administrative decisions that make usage required, and administrative support that facilitates adoption while easing change fatigue will lead to the greatest success.

Conclusion

Learning Management Systems have become a critical element in higher education and Adventist institutions are no exception. Understanding faculty perceptions can be particularly helpful when an organization is selecting a new LMS, changing to a different LMS, or upgrading an LMS to a significantly different feature set. Understanding interventions that increase the usage behavior of faculty members is a benefit for universities, their decision-makers and ultimately the students.

We believe that administrators, support staff, faculty and other stakeholders who implement the suggestions herein will find an improved understanding of faculty within Seventh-day Adventist higher education and will find ways of improving the implementation process when that time comes to improve, upgrade, and/or change the campus LMS.

David A. Jeffrey

David A. Jeffrey serves as Assistant Professor of Business at Burman University. He has been an educator and chair in business at the secondary and tertiary levels in Canada and Trinidad. His Ph.D. in Leadership is from Andrews University and his Master and Bachelor degrees are both in Business Administration.

Randy J. Siebold

Randy J. Siebold serves as Associate Professor of Leadership at Andrews University. He has spent time as an academy principal, associate superintendent, and a college academic vice-president. He received his Ph.D. in Instructional Systems Technology from Indiana University and has a Master degree in Art.

References

Ace, W., & Parker, S. (2010). Overcoming change fatigue through focused employee engagement. *OD Practitioner, 42*(1), 21-25.

Auster, E. R., & Ruebottom, T. (2013). Navigating the politics and emotions of change. *MIT Sloan Management Review, 54*(4), 31-36.

Aydin, C. C., & Tirkes, G. (2010). Open source learning management systems in distance learning. *Turkish Online Journal of Educational Technology, 9*(2), 175-184.

Bacow, L. S., Bowen, W. G., Guthrie, K. M., Long, M. P., & Lack, K. A. (2012). *Barriers to adoption of online learning systems in US higher education.* Ithaca, New York, NY.

Beatty, B., & Ulasewicz, C. (2006). Faculty perspectives on moving from Blackboard to the Moodle learning management system. *TechTrends: Linking Research & Practice to Improve Learning, 50*(4), 36-45. doi: 10.1007/s11528-006-0036-y

Boyce, M. E. (2003). Organizational learning is essential to achieving and sustaining change in higher education. *Innovative Higher Education, 28*(2), 119-136.

Brehm, J. W. (1966). *A theory of psychological reactance.* New York, NY: Academic Press.

Carter, E. (2008). Successful change requires more than change management. *Journal for Quality & Participation, 31*(1), 20-23.

Francis, R., & Shannon, S. J. (2013). Engaging with blended learning to improve students' learning outcomes. *European Journal of Engineering Education, 38*(4), 359-369.

Gautreau, C. (2011). Motivational factors affecting the integration of a learning management system by faculty. *The Journal of Educators Online, 8*(1), 1-15. https://files.eric.ed.gov/fulltext/EJ917870.pdf

Howard, S. K. (2011). Affect and acceptability: Exploring teachers' technology-related risk perceptions. *Educational Media International, 48*(4), 261-272. doi: 10.1080/09523987.2011.632275

Lewin, K. (1947). Frontiers in group dynamics: Concept, method and reality in social science; social equilibria and social change. *Human Relations, 1*(1), 5-41.

Moore, J., Dickson-Deane, C., & Gaylen, K. (2011). e-learning, online learning, and distance learning environments: are they the same? *The Internet and Higher Education, 14*, 129-135. https://www.sciencedirect.com/science/article/pii/S1096751610000886

Rogers, E. (2003). *Diffusion of innovations* (5th ed.). New York, NY: Free Press.

Schiavone, F., & MacVaugh, J. (2009). A user-based perspective on limits to the adoption of new technology. *International Journal of Technoentrepreneurship, 2*(2), 99-114.

Shannon, S., Francis, R., & Torpey, G. (2012). *Barriers to adoption of blended learning and online feedback and assessment by sessional staff.* Paper presented at the ASA 2012 Conference, Griffith University, Gold Coast, Australia.

Svanström, M., Gröndahl, F., Holmberg, J., Lundqvist, U., Svanström, M., & Arehag, M. (2012). The university and transformation towards sustainability: The strategy used at Chalmers University of Technology. *International Journal of Product Innovation Management, 31*(5), 894-907.

Talke, K., & Heidenreich, S. (2014). How to overcome pro-change bias: Incorporating passive and active innovation resistance in innovation decision models. *Journal of Product Innovation Management, 31*(5), 894-907.

Unal, Z., & Unal, A. (2011). Evaluating and comparing the usability of web-based course management systems. *Journal of Information Technology Education, 10*, 19-38.

Venkatesh, V., & Bala, H. (2008). Technology acceptance model 3 and a research agenda on interventions. *Decision sciences, 39*(2), 273-315.

Watson, W. R., & Watson, S. L. (2007). What are learning management systems, what are they not, and what should they become? TechTrends, 51 (2), 28-34. https://link.springer.com/content/pdf/10.1007/s11528-007-0023-y.pdf

10. Importance of Teaching and Instructional Design in Online Student Satisfaction

Nancy Liliana Herrera Villamizar. Coordinator of Planning and Academic Management. University of Montemorelos, Montemorelos, Mexico. Corresponding Author: lherreradec@um.edu.mx

Dora Patricia Martínez Cebreros. Coordinator of Student and Faculty Services. University of Montemorelos, Montemorelos, Mexico

Caterina Evelin Pavoni. Online Quality Assurance. University of Montemorelos, Montemorelos, Mexico

Abstract

Enrollment in online courses is increasing rapidly; however, dropout rates are still high. Some educational institutions are concerned about how to achieve their educational objectives and at the same time generate high levels of satisfaction among online students. For that reason, institutions must consider seriously the opinions of students when preparing courses with defined characteristics, in order to offer a highly positive educational experience. In this chapter a review of the literature is presented analyzing different dimensions which underlie the satisfaction of online students, particularly in relation to two important dimensions or predictors of satisfaction, namely, virtual teaching and the instructional design of the courses. When analyzing these two dimensions, we examine the existing concern about what factors favor the satisfaction of online course students. The documents on the subject were found in the databases EBSCO and Redalyc. Results suggest that the two selected predictors will play a fundamental role in the satisfaction and retention of online students.

Introduction

Online education has emerged in response to the need to facilitate access to education for those that otherwise could not be prepared academically (Allen & Seaman, 2011 cited in Burbuagh, Drape & Westfall-Rudd, 2014). As a growing trend, it is crucial for the long-term development of institutions. Due to the flexibility offered, there has been a great increase in the demand for online courses (Arjona & Cebrián, 2012; Burbuagh et al., 2014; Croxton, 2014; Erdemir, Çavdar, Bağcı, & Çorbacı, 2016; Hosler & Arend, 2012; Kauffman, 2015; Kuo, Walker, Belland, & Schroder, 2013; Sinclaire, 2012; Yelvington, Weaver, & Morris, 2012).

Despite the skepticism towards online learning, Bowen (2013) suggests that online education has demonstrated that it is effective and at the same time, economical. Online education appears to be here to stay (Cole, Shelley, & Swartz, 2014; Croxton, 2014). However, the degree of student satisfaction with this learning experience is important because it can contribute to the retention of students (Cole et al., 2014; Kane, Shaw, Sangho, Salley, & Snider, 2016; Secreto & Pamulaklakin, 2015) and can be used as a way to evaluate the effectiveness of online education. Understanding and meeting student expectations may result in higher levels of student satisfaction (Howell & Buck, 2012).

In that sense, student retention is relevant for enrollment and for maintaining the flow of institutional income. In addition, analysis of student satisfaction can point toward improvements in e-learning practices that could in turn improve student outcomes (Cole et al., 2014; Howell & Buck, 2012; Ladyshewsky, 2013; Sinclaire, 2012; Yelvington et al., 2012).

This study conceptualized and identified two of the main predictors or dimensions of online student satisfaction, providing possible categories for the development of further research. With the development and deepening of these two dimensions, we propose to improve student satisfaction with online courses through the teacher's actions and the didactic resources (or instructional design) of the course.

Methodology

This chapter is a descriptive theoretical type of documentary research. The procedure included the tracking, organization, systematization, and analysis of a set of electronic documents on the main aspects or dimensions that affect the satisfaction of a student in online mode. The units of analysis were documents all of which were found in the EBSCO and Redalyc databases.

As search criteria, the following descriptors were included: "online student satisfaction," "virtual tutoring," "professor online," "instructional design," "student satisfaction," "online student," "virtual teaching," "instructional design," "content," and "learning objects." These descriptors were combined in various ways to broaden the search criteria.

After searching for documents in each of the databases, 85 articles from between 2012 and 2017 were reviewed; 62 were selected according to the inclusion and exclusion criteria. The rejected articles did not address the desired theme or were not from peer-reviewed journals.

Student Satisfaction in the Framework of Online Education

Arjona and Cebrián (2012) define satisfaction as "the result of the difference between what I expected to happen (expectation) and what the subject says or feels having obtained (p. 94)." Similarly, Allen, Omori, Burrell, Mabry, and Timmerman (2013) and Moore and Shelton (2014), cited in Zambrano Ramírez (2016) define satisfaction as "the degree of congruence between the students' previous expectations and the results obtained, with respect to the experience of learning through virtual courses (p. 218)."

Satisfaction is an underlying indicator of success in different learning environments. Satisfied online students seem to be more committed, motivated, and achieve higher levels of learning. On the other hand, teachers seem to have much more difficulty facilitating effective learning in environments that include dissatisfied students (Dziuban et al., 2015). Therefore, student satisfaction is an important indicator of the quality of learning experiences (Kuo et al., 2013).

Importance of Studying the Satisfaction of Online Students

Satisfaction with online learning is increasingly important in higher education for a number of reasons. The most important is the rapid adoption of this modality of teaching and learning in colleges and universities. In addition, students are able to express their opinions about their experiences in formats ranging from end-of-course evaluations to social networks of all varieties, making their voice more important than ever (Dziuban et al., 2015; Sinclaire, 2012).

With the increasing availability of online education opportunities, an understanding of the factors that influence student satisfaction and student success online is vital to allow managers to attract and retain this important group of stakeholders (Kane et al., 2016; Sinclaire, 2012).

Predictors of Student Satisfaction

Online learning has redefined research on student satisfaction; this is a complex concept with very little agreement. Even the most recent factorial analytical studies have done little to resolve the lack of consensus about the dimensions that underlie satisfaction with online learning (Dziuban et al, 2015; Fernández-Pascual, Ferrer-Cascales, & Reig-Ferrer, 2013). Although the results of these studies differ in what dimensions constitute satisfaction, their objective was the same: identify the theoretical perspective underlying the student perception of online learning.

Based on the review of the literature, several dimensions were found to relate to online student satisfaction. Student satisfaction is affected by the perceived utility or convenience (Cole et al., 2014; Deveci, 2016; Dziuban et al, 2015; Erdemir et al., 2016), the clarity of instructions within the enriched learning environment (Costley & Lange, 2017; Yelvington et al., 2012), and the management of the Internet and technological tools (Deveci, 2016; Kuo et al., 2013; Marmon, Vanscoder, & Gordesky, 2014). Student satisfaction is also related to the learning experience, including the degree of interaction with the teacher and/or with other students (Burbuagh et al., 2014; Cole et al., 2014; Croxton, 2014; Fernández-Pascual et al., 2013; Kuo et al., 2013), longevity and professional development of teachers (Kane et al., 2016), and their sense of community (Marmon et al., 2014). The dimensions of their own learning abilities, including self-regulation (Kauffman, 2015), and student learning style (Kauffman, 2015; Secreto & Pamulaklakin, 2015) can also be related to online student satisfaction.

Two of the factors or dimensions which are identified frequently for student satisfaction with online learning are the instructor behaviors (teacher, instructor) (Howell, Simos & Starcher, 2016; Ladyshewsky, 2013) and instructional design (structure of the virtual course, learning resources) (Inzunza, Rocha, Márquez, & Duk, 2012; Kauffman, 2015). These findings could stimulate institutional reflection on ways to improve mentoring in the design of courses and the development of e-learning tools to increase the effectiveness of teaching and learning in online environments (Keengwe, Diteeyont, & Lawson-Body, 2012).

This section focuses on the literature that suggests satisfaction and student loyalty are affected mainly by instructor behaviors (Cole et al., 2014; Dziuban et al., 2015; Fernández-Pascual et al., 2013; Howell et al., 2016; Kane et al., 2016; Ladyshewsky, 2013) and the course design (Cole et al., 2014; Costley & Lange, 2017; Dziuban et al., 2015; Howell et al., 2016). Developing better instructional design strategies can improve the learning climate in addition to improving interaction with the content and with the teacher or instructor (Dziuban et al, 2015, Kuo et al, 2013).

Conceptualization of Virtual Teaching

Gómez (2013) proposes that the teacher's role is defined as a set of strategies focused on the effective development of student learning, by scheduling planned activities of academic advising, methodological guidance, counseling, monitoring, assessment, feedback, pedagogical interaction, and technological mediations. In online education, the teacher's role must include academic advice, including the aforementioned processes which are all important for the integral development of the student.

At the international level, research has been carried out about online student satisfaction in relation to the teacher's attention (Fernández-Pascual et al., 2013; Gómez, 2013; Howell et al., 2016; Keengwe et al., 2012; Mazurkiewicz, 2013; Padilla, Leal, Hernández, & Cabero, 2012; Perez, Martínez, & Martínez, 2015). Researchers agree that the interaction between teacher and student increases student motivation and satisfaction with their studies in the virtual modality.

Importance of Virtual Teaching in Student Satisfaction

Increased research concerning virtual and math education environments explores the relationship between online student satisfaction and attention from the teacher. The focus of this study is to discover the relationship that exists between student satisfaction and the attention of the teacher in virtual environments. Researchers have found that the relationship between teacher and student online should not be strictly academic, but should orient the student toward his personal and integral growth and help him in his self-determination (Casado, Greca, Tricio, Collado, & Lara, 2014; Guerra, 2015; E. Martínez & López, 2013; M. Martínez, Pérez, & Martínez, 2016; Silva & Astudillo, 2013). At the same time, teachers must deal with the spiritual, scientific, and behavioral needs of students. Another important aspect these authors mention is the ability of the teacher to leave positive and unforgettable traces; that is, to provoke in the student permeable experiences. This ability is closely linked to knowledge of their interests. The teacher must approach the student, taking into account his needs and expectations, in order to accompany him throughout his learning with the intention of promoting his professional and personal goals.

In the virtual realm, the teacher must bring face and closeness to the attention of their students. The human being always says something; that saying is enriched if it is given life, feeling, and good relations between teacher and student. When a teacher does not talk to anyone, s/he is not doing anything, much less teaching. The communication between teacher and student has two fundamental bases: talk to the intellect, but also talk to the heart (Prieto, 2012). On the contrary, Gutiérrez et al. (2015) think that the teacher's role aims to improve the performance of academic process, which should motivate the student to develop strategies for intellectual and autonomous learning, and collaborate with him in all academic aspects. Fernández-Pascual, et al. (2013) also point out that virtual communication and interaction between teacher and students is fundamental for the good academic performance of the student.

Moreno Almazán (2015) indicates that the interaction between students and teachers is based on more than replying to emails at a specific time, but on perceiving the presence, speed, feedback, and attention of the teacher. In addition, the teacher should encourage interaction in such a way as can reduce the feeling of isolation that some students experience. The teacher must involve all students from the beginning of the class, making the virtual environment more pleasant and encouraging spontaneity in the participation of the students themselves.

Gómez (2013) concluded that the teacher must be a facilitator, fostering the conditions for learning. Then students will be incentivized to be more autonomous and responsible for their own learning. When the level of interaction between teacher and student is higher than the student-student interaction and the student-content interaction, the degree of student satisfaction is greater (Moreno Almazán, 2015).

Aspects of Virtual Teaching that Influence Student Satisfaction Online

It should be noted that the main pedagogical benefit of the relationship between teacher and student begins with motivation and feedback, which can occur through synchronous and asynchronous means. Among the studies that demonstrate effectiveness of the teacher-student relationship, one of the elements is the importance of human interaction, which tends to increase proportionally in relation to the number of students (Moreno Almazán, 2015). This author and Lady-shewsky (2013), mention that the immediacy of the teacher-student interaction is reflected in increased cognitive development of their students in comparison with students who have less immediacy in the communication of their teachers. Deveci (2016) also suggests that teachers should have rapid and timely communication with their students through forums, chat, synchronous meetings, and constant feedback on their activities so that the students reach meaningful learning.

In addition, student satisfaction increases when the socialization between student and teacher is promoted within a virtual course, since the interaction between teacher and student will always motivate students to generate new ideas (Fuentes, 2012; Silva & Astudillo, 2013).

Instructional Design

In both online and traditional learning environments, the objectives of the course must be aligned both with the educational content and with the methods by which the learning will be evaluated, to achieve satisfactory results (Arjona & Cebrián, 2012; Jaggars & Xu, 2016; Kauffman, 2015; Ortega, 2013). This alignment is only achieved by intentional effort, through the planning and design of the course (Eom & Ashill, 2016).

Instructional design is one of the fundamental elements of the virtual environment and very influential in student satisfaction (Barbera, Clara, & Linder-Vanberschot, 2013). A poor instructional design harms learning and distracts the student with irrelevant aspects (Andrade-Lotero, 2012; Artino, 2008).

Marreros Vázquez and Amaya Amaya (2016) describe the process of instructional design as follows:

> For the delivery of any subject in the online mode, it is necessary to carry out a detailed planning of the different components to include, starting with the writing of the competencies that the student will develop and the definition of the didactic sequences necessary for the achievement of the same. The competences guide the selection of teaching resources, didactic, and assessment strategies, as well as evaluation instruments that best suit the nature of the subject and the operational level of the competency itself (p. 33).

Through instructional design, the techno-pedagogue gives precise indications about the content of learning including how it should be presented and an indication of the organization and structure that will facilitate evaluation, feedback, and motivation of the student in their learning, not as an end in itself but as the beginning of the educational process (Marreros Vázquez & Amaya & Amaya, 2016).

Instructional design includes selecting the communication tools, how they are used, at what times, and the evaluative strategies (Amaro de Chacín, Brioli, García, & Chacín, 2012); aspects of the process, participation, and interaction, as well the evaluation of the course (Eom & Ashill, 2016). A good instructional designer identifies the objectives, which activities will help achieve them, and how to evaluate them. The task is, according to Zapata-Ros (2015), to "create-search-know resources and organize them in a sequencing and progressive difficulty scheme, so there will be no jumps, discontinuities, or cognitive gaps (p. 22)."

The instructional design process defines the interaction between the teacher, the students, and the knowledge of the didactic process, in its different components (from Amaro de Chacín et al., 2012); and through the use of technology in the teaching, learning and evaluation processes, both individual and collective (Vázquez Mejía, Cisneros, & Hernández, 2012).

Instructional Design and Student Satisfaction

It is very helpful if the instructional design considers the elements that affect student satisfaction (Barbera et al., 2013; Zambrano Ramírez, 2016). Among other factors most influential is the design of the course, the content of learning, and the social presence (Barbera et al., 2013; Eom & Ashill, 2016; Gray & DiLoreto, 2016; Kauffman, 2015). When attempting to migrate their face-to-face courses to the virtual mode, ignoring certain educational pedagogical orientations of the environment, some teachers have shown insufficient competencies both in the design of a course and in providing e-moderation in a stimulating, collaborative, and socio-constructive learning environment (Amaro de Chacín et al., 2012).

Deveci (2016) found that in courses where there was interaction and the use of tools for communication (i.e. virtual classroom, forum, chat, and email), content (web pages, animation, video, graphics/images), and evaluation (questionnaire), student satisfaction was greater.

When planning an online course, care should be taken that the dialogue of the discussion fits with the student's own experiences for more meaningful learning and for promoting the "community" feeling that is lacking in some online courses (Gruenbaum, 2010; Kranzow, 2013). Providing opportunities for interaction helps students increase their overall satisfaction (Cole et al., 2014; Gray & DiLoreto, 2016).

Ilgaz and Gülbahar (2015) observed that levels of student satisfaction were affected mainly by instructional content, communication, and usability. The instructional content, the heart of learning, most influenced student satisfaction. Kuo et al. (2013) confirmed the importance of the design and organization of the content, citing similar studies (Chejlyk, 2006; Keeler, 2006) where, of the three types of interaction, content-student interaction was the strongest predictor of satisfaction of students with web-based learning. However, Ruiz and Dávila (2014) found that the high level of satisfaction of its participants did not respond to the interaction of students to content but to e-learning with "a constructivist instructional design, approached with collaborative learning strategies, with authentic tasks and socially relevant, the intermediary action of the teacher, and the active and autonomous participation of the students" (p 40).

On the other hand, Gray and DiLoreto (2016) found a relationship between the structure of the course and student satisfaction, but not between student interaction and student satisfaction. Possibly this was because the instructor used a large online community, providing few requirements for students to interact with each other, which might have caused students to interpret interaction as less important for their learning. They suggest that the findings of Kuo et al. (2013) are due to the fact that the students were postgraduate who are frequently self-motivated and might not see the importance of interacting with their peers to be satisfied.

Online learning is not successful for every student (Kauffman, 2015), but identifying the particular characteristics that contribute to the design of courses that satisfy student needs may be useful. These characteristics include adapting the content and encouraging more meaningful learning (Andrade-Lotero, 2012; Fuentes, 2012; Howell et al., 2016); creating a base for new knowledge (Barbera et al., 2013; Zapata-Ros, 2015), and facilitating as much interaction as possible (Gray & DiLoreto, 2016).

For Eom and Ashill (2016) it is essential to continuously re-educate and improve the skills and knowledge of course designers as discussion facilitators and motivators, because they are the cornerstone of the online university. Institutions must take systematic control and monitor the virtual training they offer (Amaro de Chacín et al., 2012; Gruenbaum, 2010; Kranzow, 2013) to improve quality through a scientific, reliable, and valid method (Ilgaz & Gülbahar, 2015; Martínez-Argüelles, 2013).

Conclusions

Virtual education has many advantages when the instructional design and teaching take into account factors that affect student achievement and satisfaction. This theoretical review of the literature offers a framework of analysis that helps to understand how these dimensions affect student satisfaction, with the purpose of undertaking improvements in the current and future development of virtual course designs.

The teacher's role in online courses is fundamental so that the students are highly satisfied. The teacher's role should not focus solely on the academic aspect, but should promote the integral development of students, to the benefit of their professional and personal growth.

When structuring online courses, the instructional design should be intentional in facilitating the types of interaction (student-content, student-student, and student-teacher) that have the greatest impact on student satisfaction. It is essential that institutions identify what affects student satisfaction and train their designers and teachers to provide satisfactory virtual environments. For all this, it is important to consider student satisfaction with the whole experience of learning virtually, not just the academic performance (Zambrano Ramírez, 2016), since the full experience contributes to student retention and the credibility of online education.

Nancy Liliana Herrera Villamizar

Nancy serves as an online teacher at the University of Montemorelos and Coordinator of Planning and Academic Management of the virtual UM. She graduated from the Adventist University Corporation of Colombia as a Bachelor of Education and her postgraduate work in Educational Mathematics was completed at the University of Montemorelos. She has collaborated in different teaching, research, and communication functions during her professional career.

Dora Patricia Martínez Cebreros

Patricia serves as an online teacher at the University of Montemorelos, as well as coordinator of student and teacher services in Virtual UM. She graduated from the University of Montemorelos with a Doctorate in Education. She has 20 years of experience in distance education and teaching both in person and online.

Caterina Evelin Pavoni

Caterina is an instructional and teaching designer at the Universidad de Montemorelos where she works in the area of production and evaluation of the quality of the Virtual UM courses. She graduated from the Plata Adventist School and received her postgraduate in Administration from the University of Montemorelos. She has collaborated in accounting and administrative functions and in teaching.

References

Amaro de Chacín, R.., Brioli, C., García, I., & Chacín, R. (2012). La valoración del diseño instruccional y la e-moderación en experiencias didácticas virtuales en el contexto universitario. (Spanish). *Revista De Pedagogía*, 33(92), 199-234.

Andrade-Lotero, L. A. (2012). Teoría de la carga cognitiva, diseño multimedia y aprendizaje: un estado del arte. *Magis: Revista Internacional De Investigación En Educación*, 5(10), 75-92.

Arjona Muñoz, J.A., & Cebrián de la Serna, M. (2012). Expectativas y Satisfacción de Usuarios en Cursos On Line. Estudio del Caso: Experto en Entornos Virtuales de Formación. Pixel-Bit, *Revista De Medios & Educacion*, (41), 93-107.

Artino, A.R., Jr. (2008). Cognitive load theory and the role of learner experience: An abbreviated review for educational practitioners. *AACE Journal, 16*(4), 425-439.

Barbera, E., Clara, M., & Linder-Vanberschot, J. A. (2013). Factors Influencing Student Satisfaction and Perceived Learning in Online Courses. *E-Learning and Digital Media*, 10(3), 226-235.

Bowen, W. G. (2013, March 29). Walk Deliberately, Don't Run, Toward Online Education. *Chronicle of Higher Education*. pp. A32-A33.

Burbuagh, B., Drape, T., & Westfall-Rudd, D. M. (2014). A Descriptive Account of Factors Affecting Student Satisfaction in an Online Master's Degree in Agriculture and Life Sciences. *NACTA Journal*, 58(4), 341-348.

Casado, R., Greca, I. Tricio, V. Collado, M., & Lara, A. (2014). Impacto de un plan de acción tutorial universitaria: Resultados académicos, implicación y satisfacción. *Revista de Docencia Universitaria*. 12(4). 323-342.

Cole, M. T., Shelley, D. J., & Swartz, L. B. (2014). Online Instruction, E-Learning, and Student Satisfaction: A Three Year Study. *International Review of Research in Open and Distance Learning*, 15(6), 111-131.

Costley, J. C., & Lange, C. C. (2017). The Mediating Effects of Germane Cognitive Load on the Relationship between Instructional Design and Students' Future Behavioral Intention. *Electronic Journal of E-Learning*, 15(2), 174-187.

Croxton, R. R. (2014). The Role of Interactivity in Student Satisfaction and Persistence in Online Learning. *Journal of Online Learning & Teaching*, 10(2), 314-324.

Deveci Topal, A. (2016). Examination of University Students' Level of Satisfaction and Readiness for E-Courses and the Relationship between Them. *European Journal of Contemporary Education*, 15(1), 7-23. doi:10.13187/ejced.2016.15.7

Dziuban, C., Moskal, P., Thompson, J., Kramer, L., DeCantis, G., & Hermsdorfer, A. (2015). Student Satisfaction with Online Learning: Is It a Psychological Contract? *Online Learning*, 19(2).

Eom, S. B., & Ashill, N. (2016). The Determinants of Students' Perceived Learning Outcomes and Satisfaction in University Online Education: An Update. *Decision Sciences Journal of Innovative Education*, 14(2), 185-215. doi:10.1111/dsji.12097

Erdemir, A., Çavdar, D., Bağcı, V., & Çorbacı, E. C. (2016). Factors Predicting e-Learners' Satisfaction on Online Education. *Proceedings of the Multidisciplinary Academic Conference*, 53-60.

Fernández-Pascual, M. D., Ferrer-Cascales, R., & Reig-Ferrer, A. (2013). Entornos Virtuales: Predicción de la Satisfacción en Contexto Universitario. *Pixel-Bit, Revista De Medios Y Educacion*, (43), 167-181. doi:10.12795/pixelbit.2013.i43.12

Fuentes, L. (2012). Creación de un patrón de eLearning a partir de la consideración de aspectos relacionados con el diseño de objetos de aprendizaje para un caso práctico concreto de uso del móvil para dar soporte a Lifelong Learners, desde la perspectiva del diseño instruccional. *Revista de Educación a Distancia*. No. 31.

Gómez, M. (2013). Impacto que tiene en los estudiantes la atención de la tutoría virtual, impartida por parte de tutores diplomados en tutoría virtual de la UNAD. *Revista Científica de Tecnología Educativa*. 2 (1), 104-110.

Gray, J. A., & DiLoreto, M. (2016). The Effects of Student Engagement, Student Satisfaction, and Perceived Learning in Online Learning Environments. *International Journal of Educational Leadership Preparation*, 11(1).

Gruenbaum, E. (2010). Predictors of Success for Adult Online Learners: A Review of the Literature. Retrieved from http://elearnmag.acm.org/ archive.cfm?aid=1722023

Guerra, M. (2015). La labor del tutor: una mirada desde la satisfacción de los estudiantes. *Revista de Pedagogía Universitaria*. 20(1), 15-27.

Gutiérrez, C., García, M., Pérez, C., Sahagún, A., Martínez, S., Díez, R., López, C., . . ., & Rodríguez, E. (2015). Implementación de tutorías académicas en línea en una asignatura básica del grado en veterinaria. *Revista de Docencia Universitaria*. 13, 97-121.

Hosler, K. A., & Arend, B. D. (2012). The importance of course design, feedback, and facilitation: student perceptions of the relationship between teaching presence and cognitive presence. *Educational Media International*, 49(3), 217-229. doi:10.1080/09523987.2012.738014

Howell, G., Simos, A., & Starcher, K. (2016). Is this Course worth my time? Key Factors in Adult Online Student Satisfaction. *Currents in Teaching & Learning*, 8(1), 28-39.

Howell, G. G., & Buck, J. J. (2012). The Adult Student and Course Satisfaction: What Matters Most? *Innovative Higher Education*, 37(3), 215-226. doi:10.1007/s10755-011-9201-0

Ilgaz, H., & Gülbahar, Y. (2015). A Snapshot of Online Learners: e-Readiness, e-Satisfaction and Expectations. *International Review of Research in Open and Distance Learning*, 16(2), 171-187.

Inzunza, B. C., Rocha, R. A., Márquez, C. G., & Duk, M. S. (2012). Asignatura Virtual como Herramienta de Apoyo en la Enseñanza Universitaria de Ciencias Básicas: Implementación y Satisfacción de los Estudiantes. *Formación Universitaria*, 5(4), 3-14. doi:10.4067/S0718-50062012000400002

Jaggars, S. J., & Xu, D. D. (2016). How do online course design features influence student performance? *Computers and Education*, 95, 270-284. doi: 10.1016/j.compedu.2016.01.014

Kane, R. T., Shaw, M., Sangho Pang, S., Salley, W., & Snider, J. B. (2016). Relationships among Faculty Training, Faculty Degree, Faculty Longevity, and Student Satisfaction in Online Higher Education. *Online Journal of Distance Learning Administration*, 18(4), 1-12.

Kauffman, H. T. (2015). A review of predictive factors of student success in and satisfaction with online learning. *Research in Learning Technology*, 231-13. doi:10.3402/rlt.v23.26507

Keengwe, J., Diteeyont, W., & Lawson-Body, A. (2012). Student and Instructor Satisfaction with E-Learning Tools in Online Learning Environments. *International Journal of Information & Communication Technology Education*, 8(1), 76-86. doi:10.4018/jicte.2012010108

Kranzow, J. J. (2013). Faculty Leadership in Online Education: Structuring Courses to Impact Student Satisfaction and Persistence. *Journal of Online Learning & Teaching*, 9(1), 131-139.

Kuo, Y., Walker, A. E., Belland, B. R., & Schroder, K. E. (2013). A Predictive Study of Student Satisfaction in Online Education Programs. *International Review of Research in Open and Distance Learning*, 14(1), 16-39.

Ladyshewsky, R. R. (2013). Instructor Presence in Online Courses and Student Satisfaction. *International Journal for the Scholarship of Teaching & Learning*, 7(1), 1-23.

Marmon, M., Vanscoder, J., & Gordesky, J. (2014). Online Student Satisfaction: An Examination of Preference, Asynchronous Course Elements, and Collaboration among Online Students. *Current Issues in Education*, 17(3).

Marreros Vázquez, J. J., & Amaya Amaya, A. A. (2016). Diseño de asignaturas en línea bajo el modelo por competencias para programas educativos e-Learning. (Spanish). *Campus Virtuales*, 5(2), 30-43.

Martínez Clares, P., Pérez Cusó, J. & Martínez Juárez, M. (2016). Las TICS y el entorno virtual para la tutoría universitaria. *Educación XXI*, 19(1), 287-310. doi:10.5944/educXX1.13942.

Martínez. E., & López, M. (2013). Estrategias para perfeccionar la preparación del profesor-tutor, en cuanto a su labor educativa en la carrera de contabilidad y finanzas. *EduSol* 13(43), 30-42.

Martínez-Argüelles, M. J., Blanco Callejo, M., & Castán Farrero, J. M. (2013). Las dimensiones de la calidad del servicio percibida en entornos virtuales de formación superior. (Spanish). *RUSC: Revista De Universidad Y Sociedad Del Conocimiento*, 10(1), 89-285. doi:10.7238/rusc.v10i1.1411

Mazurkiewicz, H. (2013). Análisis sistémico de la tutoría virtual a partir del auge del e-learning. *Revista Científica Electrónica de Ciencias Gerenciales*. 25(9), 114-143.

Moreno Almazán, O. (2015). Evaluación de la modalidad de interacción de la tutoría y los efectos en logro académico en entornos en línea. *RIED. Revista Iberoamericana de educación a Distancia*. 18(1), 231-255.

Ortega, E. (2013). Metodología para la elaboración de diseños instruccionales del Sistema de Educación a Distancia: caso Universidad del Zulia. *Enl@Ce: Revista Venezolana de Información, Tecnología y Conocimiento*, 10(3), 45-60.

Padilla, G., Leal, F., Hernández, M., & Cabero, J. (2012). La tutoría virtual: Un reto para el profesor del futuro. Sined. México.

Pérez Cusó, F. J., Martínez Clares, P., & Martínez Juárez, M. (2015). Satisfacción del estudiante universitario con la tutoría. Diseño y validación de un instrumento de medida. *Estudios Sobre Educacion*, 2981-3101. doi:10.15581/004.29.81-101

Prieto, D. (2012). Propuesta de principios para la práctica de la tutoría virtual. *Revista Latinoamericana de Comunicación*. 23(117), 37-40.

Ruiz Bolívar, C., & Dávila, A. (2014). Evaluación estudiantil sobre la percepción de la calidad de un curso de postgrado administrado bajo la modalidad e-learning. *Compendium*, 17 (33), 23-24.

Secreto, P. V., & Pamulaklakin, R. L. (2015). Learners' Satisfaction Level with Online Student Portal as a Support System in an Open and Distance eLearning Environment (ODeL). *Turkish Online Journal of Distance Education*, 16(3), 33-47.

Silva, J., & Astudillo, A. (2013). Formación de tutores. Aspecto clave en la enseñanza virtual. *Didáctica y Educación*. 4(1), 87-101.

Sinclaire, J. K. (2012). Vark Learning Style and Student Satisfaction with Traditional And Online Courses. *International Journal of Education Research*, 7(1), 77-89.

Vázquez Mejía, E. N., Cisneros, S. V., & Hernández, S. C. (2012). Diseño instruccional en la educación a distancia: la importancia y contribución del tecnopedagogo. *Apertura: Revista De Innovación Educativa*, 4(2), 1.

Yelvington, J. S., Weaver, D., & Morris, S. A. (2012). Student Satisfaction with Online Intermediate Accounting Courses. *International Journal of Education Research*, 7(2), 110-122.

Zambrano Ramírez, J. (2016). Factores predictores de la satisfacción de estudiantes de cursos virtuales. *RIED. Revista Iberoamericana de Educación a Distancia,* 217-235.

Zapata-Ros, M. (2015). El diseño instruccional de los MOOC y el de los nuevos cursos abiertos personalizados. *RED - Revista De Educación A Distancia*, (45), 1-35.

11. Effectiveness of E-learning: A Survey of Factors Based on Progressive Learning Theories

Prema Gaikwad. Professor, Education Department. Adventist International Institute of Advance Studies, Silang, Philippines. Corresponding Author: pgaikwad@aiias.edu

Mak Chung Yin. Senior Doctoral Student, Education Department. Adventist International Institute of Advance Studies, Silang, Philippines

Abstract

Online learning is becoming increasingly popular as an alternative modality of learning. Its development over the past few decades has been the result of a blend of progress in technology and learning theories. Even as online learning is picking up momentum in higher education, the attributes that make it a preferred choice need to be probed. Thus, this study addresses the question: What makes online learning effective? A search of the literature, specifically of learning theories which build on each other, points to four factors that are significant to online learning: (a) student autonomy, (b) instructional design, (c) interactivity, and (d) learning environment and resources. Based on these factors, a 24-item survey was administered to online students of an international institution of higher education, to find their perceptions of the effectiveness of online learning. The results indicated that all four factors are considered important for online learning to be effective. The results of this study have implications for online learners as well as course designers and facilitators of online courses in higher education.

Introduction

Online learning is a popular modality of education, as evidenced by the increase in enrollment as well as its marketability: for example, 5.8 million students in higher education (HE) had enrolled in online courses by 2016, a 263% increase in the last 12 years (Higher Education Infographics, 2016); the global market for online learning is projected to be $241 million by 2022 (Global Industry Analysts, Inc.,

2016), and is considered to be one of the most rapidly growing sectors in the education industry. However, reports exist also of high dropout rates in online courses. The dropout rate in online classes is found to be 15 to 20 percent higher than in face-to-face classes (Parry, 2010). Even as online learning continues to be a preferred choice of mainstream higher education (HE) environments, the attributes that make it effective need to be studied in various contexts and levels of education, especially in HE. This study addresses the question, "What makes online instruction effective in HE?"

This quantitative research with a survey design focused on four factors: (a) student autonomy and attitude, (b) instructional design, (c) interactivity, and (d) learning environment and resources that contribute to the effectiveness of online courses in HE, as perceived by the learners. While studies have focused on one or more of these factors, there exists a need to study all four factors in terms of online adult students' perceptions. The present study focuses on filling this gap. Using graduate online students of a selected institution of higher education in the Philippines, this study endeavored to identify factors that contribute to the effectiveness of E-learning.

The four factors used in the study are derived from an in-depth search of literature on successive learning theories that can be integrated into online learning. Following is a discussion of how the four factors were selected for the study.

Literature Review

The long history of online learning is intriguing and the resulting learning theories worth considering. The current study is based on selected learning theories derived from the historical models of distance learning and online learning. In this introductory section, a brief chronological history of online learning resulting from technological advances is presented. Then follows a description of related learning theories that were adopted into online learning.

The beginning of online learning is generally traced to the distance learning of the 1840s (Florida National University, 2014) when an English educator, Isaac Pitman, taught shorthand through correspondence. The earliest learning theories of distance learning were based on the traditional learning construct of considering students as passive recipients of information. The element of student independence or autonomy also was woven into this learning modality.

With the introduction of radio and television, distance learning took on technological tools. Although this new modality included the novelty of hearing/seeing the instructors, the learning situations lacked interaction between students and instructors, as well as interaction among students. Passive learning continued with student autonomy as an advantage.

With the electronic revolution of the 1970s, distance learning incorporated the use of computers and Internet (McDonald & Lever-Duffy, 2008; Simonson, Smaldino, Albright, & Zvacek, 2012). Distance learning branched into online learning. All along, the foundational theory of distance learning had been student autonomy.

Student autonomy in learning is promoted by experts in distance education such as Moore and Wedemeyer (as cited in Simonson et al., 2012). Due to the separation of instructor and learner, a high level of accountability and responsibility for learning rested on the learner. In such an autonomous learning context, active learning was the main approach for successful learning outcomes (Moore, as cited in Simonson et al., 2012).

Important technological communication tools were incorporated into distance learning since the 1970s. Internet-based communication through email to support one-to-one online learning was a major inclusion (Horrigan & Rainie, 2002). By 1980s, asynchronous communication technologies such as bulletin boards, Usenet News, and Internet Relay Chat (IRC) provided online discussion areas to enhance group-based online communication (Rheingold, 2000).

By 1991, Tim Berners-Lee, who enhanced the widespread usage of websites and the development of online learning, developed the World-Wide Web (WWW) (Berners-Lee, Cailliau, Groff, & Pollermann, 2010). Thereafter, streaming video, Internet telephone, web cam, open source collaborative server technology, and real-time Hyper Text editing, etc. were available to enhance online learning. Further development of smaller Internet-based devices set up a foundation for the now ubiquitous learning environment (Preece, Maloney-Krichmar, & Abras, 2003). Moodle, created in 2002, began the open-source internal network that radically changed the learning environment and access to learning resources for online learning.

With rapid technological integration into online learning, the instructional designs have changed dramatically. Online learning scholars have grappled with building a universal instructional design based on a common learning theory for online learning. But the complexity of learning situations and the varied belief systems among the stakeholders have resulted in no specific instructional design for online learning. Nevertheless, an intensification of development of learning models using appropriate technology to achieve expected learning outcomes (Mayes & de Freitas, 2007) has been observed.

In any case, reaching a consensus for a universally acceptable learning theory or instructional design for online learning is unlikely. What is possible though is a probe of the highlights of the learning theories and the resulting instructional designs from the past to the present. The result will provide a menu from which the interested party can choose the most appealing model for use in a given situation. Below is a brief overview that highlights selected online instructional designs and the related learning theories.

Instructional Designs and Learning

Theories of 1970s and 1980s

The initial online instructional designs of the 1970s were influenced by Gagne's instructional model. Gagne (1977) had suggested the waterfall instructional design model, which provided a foundation for the course design of online learning. This linear model specified three areas of learning, which are (a) learning outcomes, (b) learning conditions, and (c) a nine-step instructional event. The learning outcomes include intellectual skills, attitudes towards learning, verbal information, cognitive strategies, and motor skills. The internal conditions and external conditions form the two learning conditions. Students' capabilities and pre-existing knowledge are the internal learning conditions and the presentation of the teacher's instruction is the external learning condition.

Moreover, the nine-step instructional event of Gagne's model includes (a) gaining attention, (b) informing the learner of the objective, (c) stimulating recall of prior knowledge, (d) presenting information, (e) providing guidance, (f) eliciting performance, (g) providing feedback, (h) assessing performance, and (i) enhancing retention and transfer (Gagne, 1977). This model provides a teacher-centered instruction process and lacks students' active participation in the learning process. Similar to this waterfall model, Walter Dick, Lou Carey, and James O. Carey also developed the Dick and Carey instructional model in 1978 (Dick, Carey, & Carey, 2001). As can be expected, the instructional designs in 1970s were rigid and teacher-centered based on these models (Clark, 2015).

Independence of the learner has been an essential element of distance education from its onset and eventually of online learning as well. In the early 1970s Michael Moore formulated the theory of distance learning (also called independent study) that highlighted student autonomy, an essential feature of online learning. Moore (as cited in Simonson et al., 2012) proposed three questions that serve as guidelines to appraise the autonomy practiced in a given online course:

1. Is the selection of learning objectives in the program the responsibility of the learner or of the teacher? (autonomy in setting of objectives)
2. Is the selection and use of resource persons, of bodies and other media, the decision of the teacher or the learner? (autonomy in methods of study)
3. Are the decisions about the method of evaluation and criteria to be used made by the learner or the teacher? (autonomy in evaluation). (p. 45)

In line with Moore, Wedemeyer (as cited in Simonson et al., 2012) proposed a theory of independent study and proposed 10 attributes of student autonomy that online learning should enhance:

1. Be capable of operation anyplace where there are students—even only one student—whether or not there are teachers at the same place at the same time
2. Place greater responsibility for learning on the student
3. Free faculty members from custodial-type duties so that more time can be given to truly educational tasks
4. Offer students and adults wider choices (more opportunities) in courses, formats, and methodologies
5. Use, as appropriate, all the teaching media and methods that have been proven effective
6. Mix media and methods so that each subject or unit within a subject is taught in the best way known
7. Cause the redesign and development of courses to fit into an "articulated media program"
8. Preserve and enhance opportunities for adaptation to individual differences
9. Evaluate student achievement simply, not by raising barriers concerned with the place, rate, method, or sequence of student study
10. Permit students to start, stop, and learn at their own pace. (pp. 43, 44)

Instructional Designs and Learning

Theories of the 1990s

Laurillard's conversational model evolved from the waterfall instructional model. This interactive instructional model provided four components of learning dialogues and effective teaching. The four components include (a) student's conception, (b) student's actions, (c) teacher's conception, and (d) teacher's constructed environment. Moreover, there are four types of **dialogues** related to these four components. They are discussion, adaptation, interaction, and reflection (Laurillard, 1993).

In the discussion dialogue, interaction takes place between the teacher and the learner to ensure both agree on learning objectives. In the adaptation dialogue, adaptation takes place between the teacher's constructed environment and the learner's actions for the teacher to adapt objectives to his or her conceptions, and for students to adapt their feedback to the conception. In the interaction dialogue, interaction takes place between the environment defined by the teacher and the learner. In the reflection dialogue, reflection of the student's performance by both teacher and student allows students to reflect their learning process at all stages (Laurillard, 1993).

Basically, Laurillard's model pinpoints the interaction between various components for effective learning. Moreover, it emphasizes the importance of the active participation of students within the setting of the learning environment. This learning theory is an advancement of the waterfall instructional design.

Instructional Designs and Learning

Theories of the 2000s

A plethora of new theories of online learning emerged in 2000s. Garrison's Community of Inquiry Model, Anderson's Model of Interaction, and Ally's Model of Interaction are typical examples. All new theories are based on the essential instructional design and include various ways of interaction to enhance effective online learning. Four of the selected models discussed here are (a) Community of inquiry model, (b) Anderson's model of interaction, (c) Ally's model of interaction, and (d) Massachusetts Institute of Technology (MIT) Open Courseware and Massive Open Online Course (MOOC).

"The community of inquiry model provides a foundation for enhancing collaborative and cooperative learning in the networked e-learning environment" (Sridharan, 2011, p. 76). The three basic elements of the community of inquiry model are (a) social presence, (b) cognitive presence, and (c) teaching presence. Cognitive presence refers to "exploration, construction, resolution, and confirmation of understanding" (Garrison, Anderson, & Archer, 2001, p. 11). Social presence represents how students establish meaningful relationships among teachers and peers to obtain effective communication. Teaching presence can balance social and cognitive issues through the active instructional design and direct instruction by the teacher (Garrison, Anderson, & Archer, 2000).

The community of inquiry model not only provides a guide for active instructional design but also greatly increases types of interaction and chances of collaboration. Moreover, the learning environment and student's active participation are also emphasized.

Anderson's model of interaction is similar to the Garrison inquiry model in terms of collaboration and interactivity. However, Anderson's model emphasized six types of interaction: (a) learner to content, (b) learner to teacher, (c) learner to learner, (d) teacher to content, (e) teacher to teacher, and (f) content to content (Anderson, 2003). Learner to content interaction represents the interaction between learner and learning materials. Learner to teacher interaction allows valuable feedback for effective learning. Learner to learner interaction is the reinforcement of the learning process through peer discussion and discovery. Teacher to teacher interaction encourages teachers' professional growth among themselves. Content to content interaction touches the information exchange between systems and machines. This model of online learning integrates active instructional design, multiple interactions, students' active participation, and learning environment and resources.

Yet another model, Ally's model of interaction, suggests an effective online learning model by adding learner to interface interaction and learner to content interaction. A user-friendly and effective interface allows retrieving learning resources in a short period of time. On the other hand, learner to content interaction emphasizes the personalized retrieval of learning resources so learner can assess and evaluate the learning content easily (Berge, 2002). This model stresses the importance of learning resources, learning environment, and students' participation in addition to active instructional design and interactivity.

The recent MIT open courseware and MOOC share the same vision to provide free online courses. MIT first published 50 free courses in 2002 (MIT Open Courseware, 2017), and MOOC was formed since 2008 (MAUT, 2017). The free online course concept greatly promotes online education and attracts thousands of online educators to share their learning resources and millions of online learners to acquire knowledge through online mode. This trend reiterates that learning resources and learning environment are crucial for supporting online learning.

Summary of the Development
of Online Learning Models

In brief, the chronological development of online learning through the past decades has been phenomenal. Table 11.1 summarizes these developments and highlights the online learning attributes derived from the selected learning models.

Table 11.1 Historical Development of Online Learning

Studying the chronological development of distance learning, it is

Time-line	Online Learning Model	Student Autonomy	Instructional Design	Interactivity	Learning Environment
1970s	Gagne's Model	Passive, autonomous	Teacher-directed, rigid	Nil	Nil
	Dick and Carey Model	Passive, autonomous	Teacher-directed, rigid	Nil	Nil
1990s	Laurillard's Conversational Model	Active, autonomous	Include both teacher and students	Four dialogues	Teacher constructed environment

Time-line	Online Learning Model	Student Autonomy	Instructional Design	Interactivity	Learning Environment
2000s	Garrison's Community of Inquiry Model	Active, autonomous	Include both teacher and students	Multiple interactions	Building learning climate
	Anderson's Model of Interaction	Active, autonomous	Include both teacher and students	Six types of interactions	Building community of inquiry
	Ally's Model of Interaction	Active, autonomous	Include both teacher and students	Multiple interaction	Interaction environment

clear that at least four crucial factors exist to enhance online learning: (a) student autonomy, (b) instructional design, (c) interactivity, and (d) learning environment and resources. These four factors are used as the dimensions to survey the effectiveness of online learning in this study. Table 11.2 shows the summary of the theories, the corresponding factors, and the related sources.

Table 11.2 Theory Summary

Online Theories, Factors and Sources

Theories and Models	Factors Addressed	Literature Sources
Wedemeyer and Moore proposed the theory of independent study.	Student autonomy	Wedemeyer, 1981; Moore, 2007 (as cited in Simonson et al., 2012)
Gagne's Nine Events of Instruction, ADDIE model, and the Instructional Systems Design (ISD) model.	Instructional design	Gagne, 1977; Dick, Carey, & Carey, 2001; Leshin, Pollock, & Reigeluth, 1992
Community of Inquiry model, Borje Holmberg Theory.	Multiple types of Interactivity	Holmberg, 1986; Garrison & Anderson, 2003
The Ally's Model of Interaction, MIT Open Courseware, MOOC.	Learning environment and learning Resources	MacDonald, Stodel, Farres, Breithaupt, & Gabriel, 2001; MIT Open Courseware, 2017

The above overview of the historical development of online course designs and theories with the corresponding highlighted attributes has shed light on the theoretical framework of this study. Next is a discussion of the method and procedures used in the study.

Method

A quantitative method with the survey design was employed in conducting this study. The population consisted of 72 active online students (part-time or full-time registered during the 2017-18 school year) of the selected international institution of graduate studies. The students were international, thus representing various continents such as Africa, Asia, Europe, North America, and South America.

A survey consisting of 24 items (six items for each of the four factors) adapted from Casimiro (2009) and Sridharan (2011) was used to collect data. A Likert scale was used for the four-part questionnaire. The survey was formatted in Qualtrics for online administration. An informed consent form was emailed to all the online learners of the institution. Those students who were willing to participate in the study responded to the survey as sent through email.

During data collection, the researchers ensured confidentiality and anonymity by using the information only in the context of this study and seeking no information leading to identification of the participants. The participants were asked for voluntary participation and were not be coerced in any way to be part of the study. The response to the survey was to take less than 15 minutes.

Results

Responses came from 32 participants (44% return rate) over a period of 10 days. Data was analyzed using descriptive statistics providing the mean for each of the six questions within the four factors. Using a five-point Likert scale, the participants were asked to rate the level of agreement: for the first factor, measure ranging from Strongly Disagree to Strongly Agree, and for the other three factors, Not Effective to Very Effective. The scores were interpreted using the following criteria:

1-1.49	Strongly Disagree	Not Effective
1.5-2.49	Disagree	Somewhat Effective
2.5-3.49	Not Sure	Not Sure

3.5-4.49   Agree   Effective
4.5-5   Strongly Agree   Very Effective

Table 11.3 shows the data on Student Autonomy and Attitude (the concept of attitude was included along with autonomy) measure.

Table 11.3 Student Autonomy and Attitude Scores

The overall mean for Student Autonomy and Attitude was found to

Q No	Items	Mean	Interpretation
1	I complete assignments exactly the way my teachers tell me to do them.	4.50	Strongly agree
2	I feel very confident about my ability to learn on my own.	4.25	Strongly agree
6	I enjoy discussing my ideas about course content with other students.	4.19	Agree
4	I prefer to work by myself on assignment in my courses.	4.09	Agree
3	Online activities are interesting.	3.97	Agree
5	I study what is important to me and not always what the instructor says is important.	3.00	Agree
	Total	**4.00**	**Agree**

be 4.00, interpreted as *agree*. The result indicates positive attitude and student autonomy as a critical factor for online learning. The study concurs with the theoretical model of Moore (as cited in Simonson et al., 2012) that autonomy and attitude is an important aspect of online learning. Mehra and Omidian's (2011) study confirms this observation. In the light of Knowles's (1973) theory of andragogy, which highlights one of the characteristics of adult learners as self-directed learning, this finding befits the adult learners in the study.

Moving to the second aspect, Instructional Design, Table 11.4 presents the data related to this factor.

Table 11.4 Instructional Design Scores

Q No	Items	Mean	Interpretation
6	Course structure that is logically arranged.	4.47	Very effective
2	Clear instructions on how to participate in course learning activities.	4.25	Very effective
1	Clear communication related to course goals.	4.19	Effective
4	Opportunity to apply the knowledge created in the course to work or other non-class related activities.	4.13	Effective
3	Course activities that stimulate students' curiosity.	4.09	Effective
5	Learning activities that help students construct explanation/solutions.	4.06	Effective
	Total	**4.20**	**Effective**

The overall mean for Instructional Design was 4.20, interpreted as *effective*. Each of the six indicators of instructional design contributed to the effectiveness of online learning. Studies (Keengwe & Kidd, 2010; Rao & Tanners, 2011; Song, Singleton, Hill & Koh, 2004; Swan, 2001) have indicated the significance of various aspects included among the indicators of instructional design considered in this study. An important attribute of asynchronous course designs identified in a survey at the University of New York (as cited in Lim, 2003) was a clear and consistent course structure.

Next are findings of Interactivity within the course. Table 11.5 presents the data related to this factor.

Table 11.5 Interactivity Scores

Q No	Items	Mean	Interpretation
3	Technologies to share and learn from peers (discussion forums, email, etc.).	4.19	Effective
1	Facilities to learn by discussing relevant issues with peers.	4.16	Effective

Q No	Items	Mean	Interpretation
6	Knowledge acquisition through increased student interest.	4.09	Effective
4	Interactive learning resources (e.g. multimedia resources, self-check quizzes, etc.).	4.06	Effective
2	Facilities to learn by doing.	3.91	Effective
5	Receiving prompt feedback from online facilitators.	3.88	Effective
	Total	**4.05**	**Effective**

The mean score indicates students' perceptions of interactivity as an *effective* factor for online learning. This finding implies that through synchronous and asynchronous interactions, students feel that they are a part of the learning community. This observation supports Swan's (2001) study which pointed to the significance of interactions even in purely asynchronous online courses. Online courses having the benefits of sharing ideas and resources, interaction with peers, and interactive learning resources demonstrate outstanding traits that adult students appreciate. The findings also affirm what Lim (2003) pointed out: that a success factor was inclusion of course facilitators' active interactions with the students and dynamic discussions among students which engage the students.

Finally, the data on the fourth factor is presented. Table 11.6 shows the data on Learning Environment and Resources.

Table 11.6 Learning Environment and Resources Scores

Q No	Items	Mean	Interpretation
6	Reusability/Practicality of learning resources.	4.50	Very effective
3	Online audio/video-based lectures synchronized with lecture slides.	4.25	Very effective
2	Technology supporting management of learning sources (Moodle).	4.19	Effective

Q No	Items	Mean	Interpretation
4	Easy and fast access to learning resources (within 2 to 3 clicks).	4.16	Effective
5	Access to quality learning resources (saving time on searching and spending time on learning).	4.13	Effective
1	Facilities to access resources to match learning styles and levels.	3.94	Effective
	Total	**4.19**	**Effective**

The mean score of 4.19 indicates that overall, all the indicators of this factor are *effective*. The andragogical principles of learning (Knowles, 1973), support this finding in that adults perceive learning with applicability aspects as valuable for them. An empirical study by Areti and Bosiou-Makridou (2006) of students of an open university in Greece pointed to a similar importance of quality materials—electronic availability and accessibility of study resources. The finding of Casimiro (2009) that the online courses using "less technically demanding course tools, like the discussion forums, reading materials, and individual projects or assignments" (p. 268) were more effective also supports this observation.

Discussion

The results of the study suggest that the four factors derived from the learning theories of selected distance learning models: (a) student autonomy and attitude, (b) instructional design, (c) interactivity, and (d) learning environment and resources are perceived by adult students in HE to be important for the effectiveness of online learning. These factors were derived from successive learning theories of online learning. The results of the study provide valuable insights to stakeholders of adult online learning situations and imply the following conclusions.

The Type of Online Students

Since the participants were international students, the study gives an indication of its global application to adult online learning related to the four factors of effectiveness. In other words, these four factors identified as effective also apply to adult learners of online courses in general. The study also points to the type of students who find online learning effective: (a) those with a desire for autonomous learning and positive attitude, (b) preferably those who are practicing professionals who find immediate applications of ideas as motivating, (c) those who enjoy interactions with peers and the course facilitator, (d) those who are technologically savvy so that they can navigate the course activities and resources fluently.

Online Course Designers and Facilitators

The study confirms the need to incorporate these four critical factors contributing to effectiveness of online learning. Following a systematic course design of choice, providing a variety of learning activities that students find meaningful, and incorporating interactions and opportunities to access rich learning resources are implied. Making the students feel they belong is seen as an important element in online learning, where no direct interactions with the facilitator or peers exist. The study also points to the need for incorporating prompt feedback by the course facilitators for effective online learning.

One of the limitations of the study was the relatively small online student population and the participants available in the selected institution of HE. Also, the response time given to participants was rather short—10 days from the time the survey was sent. Any responses that came in later could not be included in data analysis.

We recommend conducting similar studies with larger populations of adult learners in HE to confirm the findings. We also recommend studying the effectiveness of these four factors among younger learners—high school and elementary levels—to see if there is a difference in the way younger learners perceive these factors. Since effective learning is the goal of all instructional endeavors, specifically online instruction, the findings of such studies will contribute to enhanced online instruction and keep dropouts to the minimum.

Finally, the researchers are intrigued by the biblical connections of this study. Jesus' model of instruction which shifted from a face-to-face modality (while He lived on earth) to a non-face-to-face modality after His resurrection and ascension, reflect the four factors for effective online instruction discussed in this study. First, the course design in terms of curriculum is the gospel message given by Jesus found in Matthew 28: 18-20 which is clear and powerful; second, the autonomy of students is brought out through the personal choices to accept the plan of salvation or not; third, interactivity is sustained through two-way communication with the "facilitators": the Holy Spirit, God the Father, and Jesus through prayer, as well as by keeping good relationships with other "students"; and fourth, learning that the resources of Scriptures, Spirit of Prophecy, and other inspirational materials are accessible and can be used. Jesus' second coming will be the graduation time for all the successful "online" learners of Jesus.

Prema Gaikwad

Prema Gaikwad is a professor in the Education Department at Adventist International Institute of Advanced Studies (AIIAS), Philippines. Her area of research interest is teaching and learning strategies including online learning. She has presented her research findings at various international conference venues and has published several articles. Her academic interest is in the areas of professional development of educators, and educational research.

Mak Chung Yin

Mak Chung Yin is currently a senior doctoral student in the Education Department at AIIAS. He was an IT director in Sam Yuk Middle School of Hong Kong from 1999 to 2004. Then he was a missionary in China from 2004 to 2014. Recently he was appointed as the education director of the Chinese Union Mission. One of his contributions is organizing the Adventist online seminary in China. His academic interest is in the areas of both Adventist online education and missiological development.

References

Anderson, T. (2003). Modes of interaction in distance education: Recent developments and research questions. In M.G. Moore & W.G. Anderson (Eds.), *Handbook of distance education* (pp. 129-144.). Mahwah, NJ: Erlbaum.

Areti, V., & Bousiou-Makridou, D. (2006). Satisfying distance students of the Hellenic Open University. *e-mentor*, 2(14).

Berge, Z. L. (2002). Active, interactive, and reflective learning. *The Quarterly Review of Distance Education, 3*(2), 181-190.

Berners-Lee, T., Cailliau, R., Groff, J. F., & Pollermann, B. (2010). Worldwide web: The information universe. *Internet Research, 20*(4), 461-471. Retrieved from http://www.emeraldgrouppublishing.com/products/backfiles/pdf/backfiles_sample_5.pdf

Clark, D. (2015). *ADDIE timeline.* Retrieved from http://www.nwlink.com/~donclark/index.html

Casimiro, L. T. (2009). Effective online instructional design as perceived by teachers and students in selected private colleges and universities. (Doctoral Dissertation), AIIAS, Philippines.

Dick, W., Carey, L., & Carey, J. O. (2001). *The systematic design of instruction* (5th ed.). New York, NY: Longman.

Florida National Univeristy. (2014). *The evolution of distance learning.* Retrieved from https://www.fnu.edu/evolution-distance-learning/

Gagne, R. M. (1977). *The conditions of learning* (4th ed.). Rinehart & Winston, NY: Holt.

Garrison, D. R., & Anderson, T. (2003). *E-learning in the 21st century: A framework for research and practice.* London, UK: Routledge Falmer.

Garrison, D. R., Anderson, T., & Archer, W. (2000). Critical inquiry in a text-based environment: Computer conferencing in higher education. *The Internet and Higher Education, 2*(2-3), 87-105.

Garrison, D. R., Anderson, T., & Archer, W. (2001). Critical thinking, cognitive presence, and computer conferencing in distance education. *American Journal of Distance Education, 15*(1), 7-23.

Global Industry Analysts, Inc. (2016). *E-learning: A global strategic business report.* Retrieved from http://www.strategyr.com/eLEARNING_Online_Education_Market_Report.asp#sthash.rSGtQB5W.dpbs

Higher Education Infographics. (2016). *The 2016 online learning landscape infographic.* Retrieved from http://elearninginfographics.com/2016-higher-education-online-learning-landscape-infographic-2/

Holmberg, B. (1986). A discipline of distance education. *International Journal of E-Learning & Distance Education*, 1(1), 25-40.

Horrigan, J. B., & Rainie, H. (2002). *Getting serious online*. Washington, DC: Pew Internet & American Life Project. Retrieved from http:// www.pewinternet.org/files/old-media//Files/Reports/2002/PIP_ Getting_Serious_Online3ng.pdf.pdf

Keengwe, J., & Kidd, T. T. (2010). Towards best practices in online learning and teaching in higher education. *MERLOT Journal of Online Learning and Teaching, 6*(2), 533-541. Retrieved from http://jolt. merlot.org/vol6no2/keengwe_0610.htm

Knowles, M. S. (1973). *The adult learner: A neglected species*. Houston, TX: Gulf.

Laurillard, D. (1993). Rethinking university teaching: A conversational framework for the effective use of learning technologies. London, England: Routledge.

Leshin, C. B., Pollock, J., & Reigeluth, C. M. (1992). *Instructional Design Strategies and Tactics*. Englewood Cliffs, NJ: Educational Technology.

Lim, J. (2003). Essentials: Structure and routines in online courses. *Journal of Adventist Education, 65*(5), 16-31. Retrieved from http://circle. adventist.org/files/jae/en/jae200365041601.pdf

MAUT. (2017). *A brief history of MOOCs*. Retrieved from https://www.mcgill.ca/maut/current-issues/moocs/history

Mayes, T., & de Freitas, S. (2007). Learning and e-learning: The role of theory. In H. Beetham & R. Sharpe (Eds.), *Rethinking pedagogy for a digital age: Designing and delivering e-learning*. London, England: Routledge Falmer.

Mehra, V., & Omnidiain, F. (2011). Attitudes towards e-learning: A case from India. *Malaysian Journal of Educational Technology, 11*(2), 13-18.

McDonald, J. B., & Lever-Duffy, J. (2008). *Teaching and learning with technology*. Boston, MA: Allyn & Bacon.

MacDonald, C. J., Breithaupt, K., Stodel, E., Farres, L., and Gabriel, M. A. (2002). Evaluation of Web-based Educational Programs: A pilot study of the Demand-Driven Learning Model. *International Journal of Testing*, 2(1), 35-61.

MIT Open Courseware. (2017). Retrieved from https://ocw.mit.edu/index. htm

Parry, M. (September 22, 2010). Preventing online dropouts: Does anything work? *The Chronicle of Higher Education*. Retrieved from https:// www.chronicle.com/blogs/wiredcampus/preventing-online-dropouts-does-anything-work/27108

Preece, J., Maloney-Krichmar, D. & Abras, C. (2003) History of online communities. In Karen Christensen & David Levinson (Eds.), *Encyclopedia of Community: From Village to Virtual World.* Thousand Oaks: Sage Publications, 1023-1027.

Rao, K., & Tanners, A. (2011). Curb cuts in cyberspace: Universal instructional design for online courses. *Journal of Postsecondary Education and Disability, 24*(3), 211-229. Retrieved from http://files.eric. ed.gov/fulltext/EJ966125.pdf

Rheingold, H. (2000). *The virtual community: Homesteading on the electronic frontier.* Retrieved from http://www.rheingold.com/vc/book/

Simonson, M., Smaldino, S., Albright, M., & Zvacek, S. (2012). *Teaching and learning at a distance: Foundation of distance education* (5th ed.). Boston, MA: Pearson.

Song, L., Singleton, E. S., Hill, J. R., & Koh, M. H. (2004). Improving online learning: Student perceptions of useful and challenging characteristics. *Internet and Higher Education, 7,* 59-70.

Sridharan, B. (2011). *Evaluating the critical success factors for sustainable e-learning ecosystems in tertiary education.* (Doctoral Thesis), RMIT University, Melbourne, Australia.

Swan, K. (2001). Virtual interaction: Design factors affecting student satisfaction and perceived learning in asynchronous online courses. *Distance Learning, 22*(2), 306-31.

Conclusion

Janine Lim. Associate Dean, Online Higher Education; Professor,.
Educational Technology. Andrews University, Berrien Springs, United
States

Anthony Williams. Director of Academic Governance and Performance,
The University of Wollongong Global Enterprises, Wollongong, Australia.
Adjunct Professor, Avondale College of Higher Education, Cooranbong,
Australia.

Adventist online education has grown significantly since the 1990s, and this collection of research shows the expansion of digital and distance education throughout the world of Adventist educational institutions. From Australia and Brazil to Mexico and the Philippines, online education in the Seventh-day Adventist church has expanded beyond North America to serve the world church with quality learning experiences.

While this book has made a significant first contribution to collective Adventist research on online learning, further research is needed. In particular, the concepts of faith integration, the Biblical foundations for learning, and making education uniquely Adventist need further research into the specific applications to the online environment. As digital tools mature and become used more commonly in global education, continued work is necessary to make connections between the blueprint for Adventist education and applications in new and existing electronic learning environments.

We hope and pray that this volume inspires you and your institutions to conduct and disseminate additional research into Adventist online, blended, and digital education.